مقدمة في أصول التفسير

لابن تيمية

AN EXPLANATION OF
SHAYKH AL-ISLAM IBN TAYMIYYAH'S

INTRODUCTION TO THE PRINCIPLES OF TAFSIR

EXPLANATION BY
SHAYKH MUHAMMAD IBN SALIH AL-UTHAYMIN

ISBN 978-1-898649-82-3

British Library Cataloguing in Publication Data.
A catalogue record for this book is available from the British Library.

Published & distributed by

Al-Hidaayah Publishing & Distribution Ltd

PO Box 3332, Birmingham B10 0UH, United Kingdom.
T: 0121 753 1889 : F: 0121 753 2422
E-mail: mail@al-hidaayah.co.uk : www.al-hidaayah.co.uk

Printed in Turkey by Mega Printing

Table of Contents

Introduction 7

The Prophet (ﷺ) Explained the Meanings of the Qur'ān to his Companions 25

Differences of Opinion amongst the Predecessors in the Exegesis of the Qur'ān.................................... 35

The Two Categories of Differences in the Exegesis of the Qur'ān Relating to the Source 81

The Second Category: Differences in *Tafsīr* Relating to Reasoning and Deductions.............................. 111

Exegesis of the Qur'ān with the Qur'ān, and Exegesis with the *Sunnah* 155

Exegesis of the Qur'ān with the Statements of the Successors (*Tābi'ūn*).. 169

Exegesis of the Qur'ān Based on Intellect 173

A Summary of '*An Introduction to the Principles of Tafsīr*' 189

Glossary 199

Publisher's Note

In the name of Allāh, the Most Gracious, the Most Merciful.

Alḥamdulillāh, it gives us great pleasure to present the new edition of *An Introduction to the Principles of Tafsīr* by the illustrious scholar, Shaykh al-Islām Ibn Taymiyyah. This new edition is now also accompanied by an explanation of the original work by the great scholar, Shaykh Muḥammad ibn Ṣāliḥ al-ʿUthaymīn. It is hoped that this explanation will better allow the reader to understand and comprehend this important work.

In order to distinguish the original text from the explanation, a two colour system has been employed throughout the book; the original text is in burgundy with the explanation in black. Whenever the original text is quoted within the explanation, this is also coloured in burgundy for ease of reading.

We ask Allāh, the Most High, to make this work beneficial and to shower His mercy upon the two authors.

Al-Hidaayah Publishing & Distribution Ltd

Chapter 1

Introduction

In the name of Allāh, the Most Gracious, the Most Merciful.

All praise is due to Allāh. We seek His assistance and His forgiveness. We seek refuge in Allāh from the evil of ourselves and the evil of our actions. Whomsoever Allāh guides none can misguide him, and whomsoever Allāh misguides none can guide him.

I bear witness that none has the right to be worshipped but Allāh alone, without partner. I bear witness that Muḥammad is His slave and Messenger. May the peace and blessings of Allāh be upon him.

This sermon is known as the *khuṭbah al-ḥājjah*. It is delivered before a person wishes to discuss a need of his, whether that need is marriage, a worldly need or a religious need. This is why it is called *khuṭbah al-ḥājjah* (the sermon of need). We shall now explain some parts of this sermon.

Whomsoever Allāh guides none can misguide him. This statement clearly shows that whomsoever Allāh has decreed guidance for none has the ability to misguide him or remove him from the guidance which he has been blessed with.

...and whomsoever He misguides none can guide him. Similarly, whomsoever Allāh has decreed misguidance for none has the ability to guide him.

I bear witness. The reason this testification is in the singular tense as opposed to the plural 'we' found at the beginning of the sermon, is due to the singular tense being more appropriate when discussing the unity and oneness of Allāh, the Most High.

I have been asked by a number of brothers to author an introduction to the exegesis of the Qur'ān, comprising of comprehensive principles which will assist one in understanding its meanings as well as differentiating between the truth and all kinds of falsehood indicating in all of the above the criterion to be used in this.

Here, the author[1] mentions the reason which led him to author this book; that reason being he was requested to do so. An author either pens a book due to him realising that there is a need for such a topic to be discussed, or there may be another reason, such as him being asked to do so. Therefore, in the first instance, he is addressing a need, and in the second he is responding to a request. Indeed, if a scholar realises that people are in need of knowledge in a particular field, then he must address this need and author works in this field. This is so that people are fully aware of the rulings and are able to worship Allāh upon clear guidance and understanding.

The author says 'comprehensive principles'. *Qawā'id* is the plural of *qā'idah* [principle] and it means the foundation of something. This is where the saying '*qawā'id al-bayt*' ['the foundations of a house'] is derived from. Therefore, these are the principles and foundations which assist one in understanding the Qur'ān and the principles of the exegesis of the Qur'ān. This is because understanding the Qur'ān is one of the three reasons for which it was revealed.

The Qur'ān was revealed for three reasons: to worship Allāh by reciting it, to understand its meanings and to act according to it. This is why the companions (ﷺ) would not pass ten verses until they had completely understood and acted upon them. They would say: 'So we learnt the Qur'ān, knowledge and action all together.'

[1] i.e. Shaykh ul-Islām Ibn Taymiyyah.

The recitation of the Qur'ān in and of itself is not too difficult; this is why it is recited by the scholar, the student and the general folk. As for understanding the Qur'ān, this requires knowledge and contemplation. The third level of acting according to its teachings is the most difficult upon a person, for one is required to strive in order to do what is necessary from believing in its teachings, then obeying its commandments and refraining from its prohibitions. Contemplate over this verse:

كِتَٰبٌ أَنزَلْنَٰهُ إِلَيْكَ مُبَٰرَكٌ لِّيَدَّبَّرُوٓا۟ ءَايَٰتِهِۦ وَلِيَتَذَكَّرَ أُو۟لُوا۟
ٱلْأَلْبَٰبِ ﴿٢٩﴾

(This is) a blessed Book which We have revealed to you, that they might reflect over its verses and that those of understanding would be reminded.

Sūrah Ṣād, 38:29

i.e. so that we may clarify to you the necessity of understanding the Qur'ān and acting according to it.

His statement 'which will assist one in understanding its meanings' emphasises that which has preceded, for the exegesis of the Qur'ān and understanding its meanings are similar to one another. It can be said that the exegesis of the Qur'ān includes its meanings, its wisdoms and mysteries, for the Qur'ān has meanings, and these meanings and rulings contain in them wisdom and mysteries. On the opposite hand, it can also be claimed that the exegesis refers to other than the meanings. The exegesis is what is apparent from the words, and the meanings refer to what is being intended. We will give some examples of this *Inshā Allāh*.

The exegesis refers to the explanation of the words, such as explaining one word by using another as is done in a dictionary. For example, in the verse:

أَوْ يَأْتِىَ
بَعْضُ ءَايَٰتِ رَبِّكَ ۗ يَوْمَ يَأْتِى بَعْضُ ءَايَٰتِ رَبِّكَ لَا يَنفَعُ نَفْسًا إِيمَٰنُهَا

...or your Lord should come or that there come some of the signs of your Lord? The Day that some of the signs of your Lord will come no soul will benefit from its faith ...

Surah al-Anʿām, 6:158

Its literal explanation would be for example: the day on which some of the signs showing the power of Allāh come..., whereas the actual intended meaning refers to the sun rising from the west. As such, here there is a difference between the literal explanation and the intended explanation. This is why the Qur'ān is explained on both fronts: a literal explanation and an explanation referring to the intended meaning, and these two explanations are sometimes synonymous and at other times they differ.

...as well as differentiating between the truth and all kinds of falsehood. The author mentions here that the exegesis of the Qur'ān is of two types: that which is taken from religious sources and that which is taken from the intellect. However, it is important that the second type (intellectual) does not contradict the first type, due to textual exegesis having precedence over intellectual exegesis. The reason for this precedence is that the intellect can sometimes be overcome with doubts and desires which prevent it from reaching the truth, whereas this is not the case with religious sources. It should also be noted that religious texts can at times also possess weak narrations, such as Israelite traditions, or weak and fabricated *ḥadīths*, all of which are present in some works of *tafsīr*. Therefore, it is important to know how to differentiate between the truth and all kinds of falsehood.

Indicating in all of the above the criterion to be used in this. This criterion can either be taken from religious texts or from the intellect, for intellectual proof can be used when explaining the Qur'ān so long as it does not oppose religious texts. If this is borne in mind, there is no doubt that the intellect has a great bearing in understanding the Qur'ān. It is for this reason that Allāh orders us in many verses of the Qur'ān to contemplate and to think. Rather in the statement of Allāh ***"that they may reflect over its verses,"*** there is a clear indication showing that this reflection is achieved by the human intellect.

The books of Qur'ānic exegesis contain both good and bad, apparent falsehood and clear truth. Knowledge is either a text which is received from an infallible source, or a saying backed by a clear proof. As for all else, then it is either false and rejected, or doubtful so its truthfulness or falsehood cannot be ascertained.

Knowledge is either a text which is received from an infallible source, meaning the Prophet (ﷺ). Or a saying backed by a clear proof, referring to the sayings of the companions, their students (*tābiʿūn*) and subsequent scholars. However, these sayings must be supported by evidences from religious texts or intellectual proofs; for this reason we accept analogy (*qiyās*) as evidence.

The above should also be taken as a general principle for real knowledge. Knowledge is based upon texts received from an infallible source, or a saying supported by evidence. All else is either false and thereby rejected or doubtful and as such we remain silent regarding its authenticity or lack thereof. This paragraph [of the author's] also has a certain rhythmical tone to it, and so long as this is not overdone then without a doubt this tone beautifies the speech. This is why it can also be found at times in the speech of the Prophet (ﷺ).

As for all else - This refers to everything else apart from a text received from an infallible source or a saying supported by evidence. Then it is either false and rejected - This is mentioned here as being the opposite to a text received from an infallible source. Or doubtful so its truthfulness or falsehood cannot be ascertained. This means we remain silent concerning it.

In conclusion, there are three categories: the first is that which you know to be authentic. The second is that which you know to be false. The third is that which one remains silent on, due to there being no clear indication showing whether it is from the first or second category. Therefore, the first category is accepted. The second is rejected and the third is not judged.

The Muslim Nation (*Ummah*) greatly needs to understand the Qur'ān which is the firm rope of Allāh, the wise reminder and the straight path. Evil desires will never corrupt it. Wicked tongues will never distort it. Continuously studying it will never cause it to fade and its miracles will never cease.

Here the author (may Allāh have mercy upon him) comments that people are in need of understanding the Book of Allāh. This is something clear and apparent for they have been ordered to follow this Book. Were a person ordered to follow a book written by a man he would need to study and familiarise himself with it. What then, if this is the Book of Allāh, the Most High?

The author then uses a number of attributes with which he describes the Qur'ān. He says: Which is the firm rope of Allāh. It is the firm rope of Allāh, as He is the one who revealed it. The word rope (*ḥabl*) linguistically refers to that which is used in order to reach something or somewhere else. Furthermore, it is mentioned as being the rope of Allāh as it leads to Him.

The second description is 'the wise reminder'. This description is taken from the verse:

ذَٰلِكَ نَتْلُوهُ عَلَيْكَ مِنَ ٱلْءَايَٰتِ وَٱلذِّكْرِ ٱلْحَكِيمِ ﴿٥٨﴾

This is what We recite to you, [O Muḥammad], of [Our] verses and the precise [and wise] message [i.e. the Qur'ān].

Sūrah Āl-'Imrān, 3:58

So the Qur'ān is a reminder and an honour for those who hold onto it and recite it.

وَإِنَّهُۥ لَذِكْرٌ لَّكَ وَلِقَوْمِكَ

And indeed, it is a remembrance for you and your people.

Sūrah al-Zukhruf, 43:44

This refers to it being an honour. It is also wise as it contains in its rulings and teachings ultimate wisdom. And the straight path, i.e. a path which is not crooked.

Evil desires will never corrupt it. No matter how great the evil desires of mankind are they will never corrupt it. Rather, it is complete and everlasting despite all efforts to corrupt it. It is guidance.

Wicked tongues will never distort it. The Qur'ān was revealed in the pure Arabic language and so can never be distorted. Even non-Arabs recite it in Arabic which is why the words of the Qur'ān can never be translated.[2]

Continuously studying it will never cause it to fade. Irrespective of how many times it is repeated, it is as if one has never read it. On the other hand, if one was to repeatedly read a poem or sermon written by the most eloquent person it would eventually become boring. Even though certain chapters of the Qur'ān are often repeated in a single prayer one does not become fed up with them. This is from the great signs of Allāh present in the Qur'ān.

And its miracles will never cease. This is for the one who has been granted understanding of the Qur'ān; he is able to appreciate its great and hidden meanings. As for the one who turns away from it, he may never witness a single miracle in it. So here the description is of the Qur'ān and not the reciter.

[2] Translator's note: The available translations of the Qur'ān are translations of the meanings. The miracle of the Qur'ān is such that it is unique in its language and eloquence and so cannot be directly translated.

The scholars will never be able to reach its depths. Whoever utters it has spoken the truth. Whoever acts according to it will be rewarded. Whoever rules by it has been just. Whoever calls to it has been guided to the straight path. And whosoever arrogantly leaves it will be destroyed. And whosoever seeks guidance elsewhere will be misguided.

All of the above descriptions hold true; the one who ponders will realise this. The scholars will never be satisfied that they have studied it sufficiently. The more a person learns about Allāh and His religion the more he loves the Qur'ān. You find such a person constantly pondering and contemplating over the Qur'ān, whilst studying or walking, at any time or place.

Also, whoever utters it has spoken the truth. This is because it is the most truthful and honest of speech. If for example, a person says that the disbelievers in the Hereafter will be in the Hellfire, he has spoken the truth, as this is what is mentioned in the Qur'ān.

Whoever acts according to it will be rewarded, i.e. he will be rewarded for his actions.

Whoever rules by it has been just. This applies to general rulings or rulings between people. So, if one were to say: 'dead animals are unlawful to eat'[3] then he is just, as this and other rulings are to be found in the Qur'ān. Whoever says:

فَمَنِ ٱعْتَدَىٰ عَلَيْكُمْ فَٱعْتَدُوا۟ عَلَيْهِ بِمِثْلِ مَا ٱعْتَدَىٰ عَلَيْكُمْ

So whoever has assaulted you, then assault him in the same way that he has assaulted you.

Sūrah al-Baqarah, 2:194

Such a person has also spoken the truth.

---

[3] Translator's note: This is referring to those animals that have died without being sacrificed.

Whoever calls to it has been guided to the straight path. This means that Allāh has guided such an individual, for one who calls to the Qur'ān has been guided to the straight path. As for one who calls to his own desires then he will be misguided. This is why the author also states: And whosoever seeks guidance elsewhere will be misguided.

And whosoever arrogantly leaves it will be destroyed. This peril and destruction does not necessarily have to take place in this world, but it can also be in the Hereafter.

Allāh says:

فَإِمَّا يَأْتِيَنَّكُم مِّنِّي هُدًى
فَمَنِ ٱتَّبَعَ هُدَايَ فَلَا يَضِلُّ وَلَا يَشْقَىٰ ﴿١٢٣﴾ وَمَنْ أَعْرَضَ عَن
ذِكْرِي فَإِنَّ لَهُۥ مَعِيشَةً ضَنكًا وَنَحْشُرُهُۥ يَوْمَ ٱلْقِيَٰمَةِ
أَعْمَىٰ ﴿١٢٤﴾ قَالَ رَبِّ لِمَ حَشَرْتَنِيٓ أَعْمَىٰ وَقَدْ كُنتُ بَصِيرًا ﴿١٢٥﴾
قَالَ كَذَٰلِكَ أَتَتْكَ ءَايَٰتُنَا فَنَسِيتَهَا ۖ وَكَذَٰلِكَ ٱلْيَوْمَ تُنسَىٰ ﴿١٢٦﴾

And if there should come to you guidance from Me – then whoever follows My guidance will neither go astray [in the world] nor suffer [in the Hereafter]. And whoever turns away from My remembrance – indeed, he will have a depressed [i.e. difficult] life, and We will gather [i.e. raise] him on the Day of Resurrection blind. He will say, "My Lord, why have you raised me blind while I was [once] seeing?" [Allāh] will say, "Thus did Our signs come to you, and you forgot [i.e. disregarded] them; and thus will you this Day be forgotten."

Sūrah Ṭā-Hā, 20:123-126

...will neither go astray [in the world] nor suffer [in the Hereafter]. This verse means that he will not go astray regarding his knowledge, nor will he suffer in his actions. Another explanation is he will not go astray in this world, nor will he suffer in the Hereafter, and each interpretation alludes to the other. However, misguidance is normally referred to as being the opposite of knowledge and guidance, and suffering is the opposite of happiness.

And whoever turns away from My remembrance – indeed, he will have a depressed [i.e. difficult] life, and We will gather [i.e. raise] him on the Day of Resurrection blind. It is said that a 'depressed life' refers to the punishment of the grave; the grave will continue to constrict until one's body is twisted. Others state that this 'depressed life' will be in this world, and even though he may apparently show signs of happiness, his heart will be in a state of depression and constriction. Allāh says:

فَمَن يُرِدِ ٱللَّهُ أَن يَهْدِيَهُۥ يَشْرَحْ صَدْرَهُۥ لِلْإِسْلَٰمِ ۖ وَمَن يُرِدْ
أَن يُضِلَّهُۥ يَجْعَلْ صَدْرَهُۥ ضَيِّقًا حَرَجًا كَأَنَّمَا يَصَّعَّدُ
فِى ٱلسَّمَآءِ ۚ

So whoever Allāh wants to guide – He expands his breast to [contain] Islām; and whoever He wants to misguide – He makes his breast tight and constricted as though he were climbing into the sky.

Sūrah al-Anʿām, 6:125

He, the Most High, also states:

مَنْ عَمِلَ صَٰلِحًا مِّن ذَكَرٍ أَوْ أُنثَىٰ وَهُوَ مُؤْمِنٌ فَلَنُحْيِيَنَّهُۥ
حَيَوٰةً طَيِّبَةً ۖ

Whoever does righteousness, whether male or female, while he is a believer – We will surely cause him to live a good life.

Sūrah al-Naḥl, 16:97

This last verse shows that whoever's condition is not as mentioned then their life will not be good and pleasant.

...and We will gather [i.e. raise] him on the Day of Resurrection blind. This blindness is both literal and metaphorical. This is why such a person will question:

"My Lord, why have you raised me blind while I was [once] seeing?" [Allāh] will say, "Thus did Our signs come to you and you forgot [i.e. disregarded] them", meaning you ignored them and chose not to act according to them. As a result of that: and thus will you this Day be forgotten.

The point being made here is that in holding fast to the Qur'ān one achieves happiness in this life and the next, and the one holding onto it will neither go astray nor will he suffer. On the other hand, turning away from it is a cause of depression and sorrow in this world and in the Hereafter.

And He says:

قَدْ جَآءَكُم مِّنَ ٱللَّهِ نُورٌ وَكِتَٰبٌ
مُّبِينٌ ﴿١٥﴾ يَهْدِى بِهِ ٱللَّهُ مَنِ ٱتَّبَعَ رِضْوَٰنَهُۥ
سُبُلَ ٱلسَّلَٰمِ وَيُخْرِجُهُم مِّنَ ٱلظُّلُمَٰتِ إِلَى
ٱلنُّورِ بِإِذْنِهِۦ وَيَهْدِيهِمْ إِلَىٰ صِرَٰطٍ مُّسْتَقِيمٍ

...there has come to you Our Messenger making clear to you much of what you used to conceal of the Scripture and overlooking much.[4] *There has come to you from Allāh a light and a clear Book [i.e. the Qur'ān]. By which Allāh guides those who pursue His pleasure to the ways of peace and brings them out from darkness into the light, by His permission, and guides them to a straight path.*

Sūrah al-Mā'idah, 5:15-16

This Qur'ān is divine revelation and it is the cause for guidance by the permission of Allāh. The one who is guided by it is he who pursues that which pleases Allāh, as Allāh says:

هُدًى لِّلْمُتَّقِينَ ﴿٢﴾

A guidance for those who are conscious of Allāh [i.e. have piety]

Sūrah al-Baqarah, 2:2

And Allāh says:

يَٰٓأَيُّهَا ٱلنَّاسُ قَدْ جَآءَتْكُم مَّوْعِظَةٌ
مِّن رَّبِّكُمْ وَشِفَآءٌ لِّمَا فِى ٱلصُّدُورِ وَهُدًى وَرَحْمَةٌ لِّلْمُؤْمِنِينَ

O mankind, there has come to you instruction from your Lord and healing for what is in the breasts and guidance and mercy

[4] i.e. of your sin in that regard.

for the believers.
Sūrah Yūnus, 10:57

In the second of the two verses mentioned by the author, Allāh says: By which Allāh guides those who pursue His pleasure to the ways of peace. He mentions ways or paths (*subul*) as a plural even though there is only one path which leads to Him, as is mentioned in the verse:

وَأَنَّ هَٰذَا صِرَٰطِي مُسْتَقِيمًا فَٱتَّبِعُوهُ ۖ وَلَا تَتَّبِعُوا۟ ٱلسُّبُلَ
فَتَفَرَّقَ بِكُمْ عَن سَبِيلِهِۦ ۚ

And, [moreover], this is My path, which is straight, so follow it; and do not follow [other] ways; for you will be separated from His way.
Sūrah al-Anʿām, 6:153

Therefore the correct way to combine the two verses is to say: The true path is only one. However it is divided into branches and divisions, such as the prayer, charity, fasting, pilgrimage, *jihād*, being good to others, joining the ties of kinship and so on. These are many smaller paths which all merge into one main path. We also don't say 'paths' [in the plural] when referring to Islām. Rather an adjective is attached showing the intended meaning, as is done in the verse: 'the ways of peace.' The ways of peace refer to Islām.

...and brings them out from darkness into the light. This is metaphorical. The darkness referred to here is a darkness of ignorance and intent. The darkness of ignorance points to that person who has no knowledge, and the darkness of intent refers to the one who possesses knowledge but does not wish to believe in it and act according to it. Opposing that is the light of knowledge and action.

الٓرۚ كِتَٰبٌ أَنزَلۡنَٰهُ إِلَيۡكَ لِتُخۡرِجَ ٱلنَّاسَ مِنَ ٱلظُّلُمَٰتِ
إِلَى ٱلنُّورِ بِإِذۡنِ رَبِّهِمۡ إِلَىٰ صِرَٰطِ ٱلۡعَزِيزِ ٱلۡحَمِيدِ ﴿١﴾
ٱللَّهِ ٱلَّذِي لَهُۥ مَا فِي ٱلسَّمَٰوَٰتِ وَمَا فِي ٱلۡأَرۡضِۗ

Alif Lām Rā. [This is] a Book which We have revealed to you, [O Muḥammad], that you might bring mankind out of darkness into the light by permission of their Lord – to the path of the Exalted in Might, the Praiseworthy. Allāh, to whom belongs whatever is in the heavens and whatever is on the earth.

Sūrah Ibrāhīm, 14:1-2

These verses are similar to the previous in their meaning, but there is an added benefit to be derived here. That benefit is the validity of ascribing something to its known cause, as is in the verse: that you might bring mankind out, referring to the Prophet (ﷺ). This is stated even though the One who truly brings them out of this darkness is Allāh, which is why He adds: by permission of their Lord, in order to ensure that everyone knows that the cause (i.e. the Prophet (ﷺ)) does not achieve the desired result of his own accord.

Therefore, to ascribe something to its known cause is permissible. This is mentioned in both the Qur'ān and the *Sunnah*. This is allowed so long as that cause is known through the *sharīʿah* or can be witnesses or sensed. However, it is important to note that when one believes in these causes he must also believe that these causes have no power in and of themselves, but rather they exist with the permission of Allāh.

...the Praiseworthy, i.e. that Allāh is deserving of all praise for His attributes and actions, and He praises His servants who are worthy of such praise.

Allāh says:

وَكَذَٰلِكَ أَوْحَيْنَآ إِلَيْكَ رُوحًا مِّنْ أَمْرِنَا ۚ مَا كُنتَ تَدْرِى مَا ٱلْكِتَٰبُ
وَلَا ٱلْإِيمَٰنُ وَلَٰكِن جَعَلْنَٰهُ نُورًا نَّهْدِى بِهِۦ مَن نَّشَآءُ مِنْ عِبَادِنَا ۚ
وَإِنَّكَ لَتَهْدِىٓ إِلَىٰ صِرَٰطٍ مُّسْتَقِيمٍ ﴿٥٢﴾ صِرَٰطِ ٱللَّهِ ٱلَّذِى لَهُۥ
مَا فِى ٱلسَّمَٰوَٰتِ وَمَا فِى ٱلْأَرْضِ ۗ أَلَآ إِلَى ٱللَّهِ تَصِيرُ ٱلْأُمُورُ ﴿٥٣﴾

And thus We have revealed to you an inspiration of Our command [i.e. the Qur'ān]. You did not know what is the Book or [what is] faith, but We made it a light by which We guide whom We will of Our servants. And indeed, [O Muḥammad], you guide to a straight path. The path of Allāh, to whom belongs whatever is in the heavens and whatever is on the earth. Unquestionably, to Allāh do [all] matters evolve [i.e. return].

Sūrah al-Shūrā, 42:52-53

I have written this introduction and made it brief, full of beneficial points by the blessing of Allāh. Allāh alone guides to the path of righteousness.

And thus We have revealed to you an inspiration of Our command. The inspiration here refers to the Qur'ān. It is called an inspiration because it is the source of life for the heart and soul, and for the body too. The one who is guided by it will enjoy a complete life in this world and the Hereafter.

...an inspiration of Our command, i.e. that which We command and reveal. This is also a proof that the Qur'ān is not created, as Allāh mentions in another verse:

أَلَا لَهُ ٱلْخَلْقُ وَٱلْأَمْرُ ۗ

Unquestionably, His is the creation and the command

Sūrah al-A'rāf, 7:54

In this verse Allāh separates the creation from His command, and as mentioned in the previous verse the Qur'ān is from the command and not the creation. As such the Qur'ān is not created.

You did not know what is the Book or [what is] faith. This means the Prophet (ﷺ) was not aware of what the Book or faith was before he received divine revelation.

...but We made it a light by which We guide whom We will of Our servants. This inspiration we cause to inspire and become a guiding light for those who We wish to guide from Our servants. 'Servants' is a general term signifying that it is not known whom Allāh wishes to guide by this Qur'ān. However, one of the previous verses mentioned by the author indicates that they are those who seek Allāh's pleasure.

And indeed, [O Muḥammad], you guide to a straight path. Notice how in the first part of this verse Allāh says 'We guide' and at the end of this verse how He states 'you guide'. The difference between the two forms of guidance is that the Prophet (ﷺ) shows the way, like a guide upon a path, but it is Allāh who gives that person the ability to seek guidance in the first place. So the Prophet (ﷺ) guides to Allāh, but he does not choose whom he guides, as Allāh says:

إِنَّكَ لَا تَهْدِى مَنْ أَحْبَبْتَ

Indeed, [O Muḥammad], you do not guide whom you like
Sūrah al-Qaṣaṣ, 28:56

Rather, the Prophet (ﷺ) guides to the straight path.

The path of Allāh, to whom belongs whatever is in the heavens and whatever is on the earth. In this verse the path is described as belonging to Allāh, whereas in *Surah al-Fātiḥah* the path is described as being ***'The path of those upon whom You have bestowed favour'***. There is no contradiction between the two.

It is the path of Allāh as He is the One who placed it and it ultimately leads to Him. It is also referred to as being the path of the people as they are the ones who tread upon it. Hence, both descriptions are correct each in their own context.

Unquestionably, to Allāh do [all] matters evolve [i.e. return]. In this verse 'matters' means all the affairs of this life and the next; religious and worldly. All of these affairs will return to Allāh. For this reason, there is no respite for the creation except in turning to their Lord in all of their affairs. Allāh says:

وَمَا ٱخْتَلَفْتُمْ فِيهِ مِن شَىْءٍ فَحُكْمُهُۥٓ إِلَى ٱللَّهِ

And in anything over which you disagree – its ruling is [to be referred] to Allāh
Sūrah al-Shūrā, 42:10

Regarding the worldly affairs, Allāh says:

قُلْ مَنۢ بِيَدِهِۦ مَلَكُوتُ كُلِّ شَىْءٍ وَهُوَ يُجِيرُ وَلَا يُجَارُ
عَلَيْهِ إِن كُنتُمْ تَعْلَمُونَ ﴿٨٨﴾ سَيَقُولُونَ لِلَّهِ

Say, "In whose hand is the realm of all things – and He protects while none can protect against Him – if you should know?" They will say, "[All belongs] to Allāh."
Sūrah al-Mu'minūn, 23:88-89

The word *alā* [unquestionably] in Arabic emphasises that these affairs return to Allāh alone and to none else.

I have written this introduction and made it brief, full of beneficial points by the blessing of Allāh. Allāh alone guides to the path of righteousness.

CHAPTER 2

The Prophet (ﷺ) Explained the Meanings of the Qur'ān to his Companions

It is obligatory to know that the Prophet (ﷺ) explained to his companions the meanings of the Qur'ān just as he taught its words. The following statement of Allāh includes both:

لِتُبَيِّنَ لِلنَّاسِ مَا نُزِّلَ إِلَيْهِمْ

...that you may make clear to the people what was sent down to them
Sūrah al-Naḥl, 16:44

Similar to this verse is another:

ثُمَّ إِنَّ عَلَيْنَا بَيَانَهُۥ ﴿١٩﴾

Then upon Us is its clarification [to you].
Sūrah al-Qiyāmah, 75:19

This verse also includes both aspects: teaching its meanings as well as its words. In this there is a clear refutation against those who claim that the Prophet (ﷺ) did not explain the Names and Attributes of Allāh. This claim implies that the Prophet (ﷺ) is either ignorant and did not know the meanings, or he knew the meanings but did not reveal them thus deceiving the people.

Abū ʿAbdul-Raḥmān al-Sulamī[5] said: "It has been related to us by those who used to teach us to read the Qur'ān, the likes of ʿUthmān ibn ʿAffān, ʿAbdullāh ibn Mas'ūd[6] and other than them, that when learning from the Prophet (ﷺ) they would not proceed past ten verses until they had learnt what was contained in them of knowledge and action. They said: 'So we learnt the Qur'ān, knowledge and action all at once.'[7] This is why it would take them some time to memorise a single *sūrah*."

Anas[8] said: "If a man from amongst us was able to memorise *Baqarah* and *Āl-ʿImrān* he would gain respect in our eyes."[9]

Such a person would be greatly respected among them, for they would not memorise anything they had not understood. If such a person had memorised both the words and meanings of *Baqarah* and *Āl-ʿImrān*, he would have truly amassed a great amount of knowledge.

[5] Abū ʿAbdul-Raḥmān ʿAbdullāh ibn Ḥabīb al-Sulamī, an eminent successor (*tābiʿī*) of Kūfah and a reliable transmitter of *ḥadīth*.

[6] Abū ʿAbdul-Raḥmān ʿAbdullāh ibn Masʿud, died 32 AH. He was one of the earliest six to embrace Islām and was in the service of the Prophet for many years. He was the most knowledgeable companion on the Qur'ān. ʿUmar, the second Caliph, sent him to Kūfah to teach Qur'an, where he also served as a judge.

[7] Collected by Ibn Abū Shaybah, vol. 6, p. 117.

[8] Anas ibn Mālik, died 93 AH. One of the ten most prolific transmitters of *ḥadīth*, he entered the service of the Prophet as a young boy and was with him for ten years.

[9] *Musnad Aḥmad*.

Ibn ʿUmar[10] spent a number of years – it is said eight years – in the memorisation of *Sūrah al-Baqarah*. This is reported by Mālik.[11] All of this is as a result of the saying of Allāh:

كِتَٰبٌ أَنزَلْنَٰهُ إِلَيْكَ مُبَٰرَكٌ لِّيَدَّبَّرُوٓا۟ ءَايَٰتِهِۦ وَلِيَتَذَكَّرَ أُو۟لُوا۟ ٱلْأَلْبَٰبِ ﴿٢٩﴾

(This is) a blessed Book which We have revealed to you, that they might reflect over its verses and that those of understanding would be reminded.
Sūrah Ṣād, 38:29

And His statements:

أَفَلَا يَتَدَبَّرُونَ ٱلْقُرْءَانَ

Then do they not reflect upon the Qur'ān
Sūrah Muḥammad, 47:24

أَفَلَمْ يَدَّبَّرُوا۟ ٱلْقَوْلَ

Then have they not reflected over the word
Sūrah Mu'minūn, 23:68

Therefore it is not possible to contemplate over the Qur'ān without first understanding its meanings. Allāh, the Most High, also says:

إِنَّآ أَنزَلْنَٰهُ قُرْءَٰنًا عَرَبِيًّا لَّعَلَّكُمْ تَعْقِلُونَ ﴿٢﴾

Indeed, We have sent it down as an Arabic Qur'ān that you might understand
Sūrah Yūsuf, 12:2

[10] ʿAbdullāh ibn ʿUmar ibn al-Khaṭṭāb, died 74 AH. He was one of the most outstanding young companions, and a learned scholar known for his piety and strict imitation of Prophetic practices. He distinguished himself as a narrator of *ḥadīth*, next only to the most prolific narrator, Abū Hurayrah.

[11] *Muwatta Mālik*, p. 205. Mālik ibn Anas, died 179 AH. He was the founder of the Mālikī school of *fiqh* and was the leading scholar of *ḥadīth* of Madīnah in his time.

(This is) a blessed Book which We have revealed to you, that they might reflect over its verses. The blessing of the Qur'ān is in its recitation, its comprehension and acting according to it. Likewise, its blessings extend to the effect it has upon the heart in increasing faith (*īmān*), learning about Allāh, His names, attributes and rulings. Likewise, it includes the effects it has upon nations, as it has opened the east and the west. Those who hold onto it gain honour and power over all others, as well as possessing pure intentions, a correct methodology and happiness in this world and the Hereafter. Thus, the Qur'ān has many blessings which cannot be enumerated.

...that they might reflect over its verses and that those of understanding would be reminded. In the conclusion of this verse there is praise for the one whom the Qur'ān is a reminder; such a person is praised as having intelligence.

Then do they not reflect upon the Qur'ān. This verse encourages reflecting over the Qur'ān, for Allāh has censured those who do not ponder over it. Then have they not reflected over the Word. 'The Word' here is also referring to the Qur'ān. The remainder of this verse continues: ***"Then have they not reflected over the Word [i.e. the Qur'ān], or has there come to them that which had not come to their forefathers? Or did they not know their Messenger, so they are towards him disacknowledging?"***

Indeed, We have sent it down as an Arabic Qur'ān that you might understand. The Qur'ān was revealed in the Arabic language so that the Arabs could understand and comprehend it. Were it to have been revealed in a foreign language it would not have been understood.

It is well known that the purpose of speech is not just to understand the words being spoken, but the intended meanings behind those words too. If this is the case with normal speech, then the Qur'ān is more befitting of this. Likewise, it is also the custom of people when they are studying in a certain field such as medicine or mathematics that they seek to understand it. This is more so with the speech of Allāh which is their source of protection, success and happiness, as well as the backbone of their worldly and religious affairs.

This is true. If for example, we were to take the book *Zād al-Mustaqni'*[12] and just read it without seeking to understand it we would not benefit much. Similarly, if we were to just simply read books on medicine or chemistry without understanding them, again the benefit would be minimal. For this reason, whenever people read such books they seek to understand them and have them explained.

The Qur'ān does not differ in this respect just because one is rewarded for its recitation. Rather, the Qur'ān has two sides to it, the first being an act of worship and the second being to implement its teachings. The first can be achieved by reciting the Qur'ān. The second includes the reason for which it was revealed:

لِّيَدَّبَّرُوٓا۟ ءَايَٰتِهِۦ وَلِيَتَذَكَّرَ أُو۟لُوا۟ ٱلْأَلْبَٰبِ ﴿٢٩﴾

...that they might reflect over its verses and that those of understanding would be reminded

This aspect is lost if a person does not understand the meanings of the Qur'ān.

[12] Translator's note: A *fiqh* text based upon the Ḥanbalī school of law.

For this reason, the companions rarely differed regarding the exegesis of the Qur'ān. This difference occurred more in the time of their students (*tābiʿūn*) but was still considerably less when compared to later generations. In short, the more noble a generation was, the more profound their knowledge, understanding and unity.

The companions rarely differed over the exegesis of the Qur'ān due to two reasons:

The First: The Qur'ān was revealed in their pure language during their time, so they best understood its meanings. Then, over time people's understanding of the language changed.

The Second: Their intentions were sincere and pure. None of them were trying to gain support for their own causes or ideas. Rather, each one of them would support the truth no matter where he found it, to the extent, that the leader (*khalīfah*) would change his ruling based upon the truth a woman would remind him of. He would not unjustly claim that because he was the ruler he may do as he pleases. For these two reasons the companions differed little in their understanding of the speech of Allāh.

During the time of their students, the *tābi'ūn*, the two above reasons were still present. What changed was that during this time many lands were conquered, and as a result Arabic and foreign languages mixed. This is why it has been mentioned that the first authorial work in Arabic grammar (*naḥw*) took place during the time of ʿAlī (رضي الله عنه).

At the same time, people's desires increased and trials became rife. People began to call to their own ideas and theories, to the extent that fighting and killing occurred between the Muslims. For this reason, they differed more than the companions did. The further the generations became from the time of prophethood, the greater the trials which struck them and the more visible the confusion between truth and falsehood. As we witness in our time, every mosque has a scholar who considers himself to be Ibn Taymiyyah, and every camp in Mina possesses someone who believes he is Aḥmad ibn Ḥanbal or al-Shāfiʿī!

Due to this, you will find that a religious matter which previously had one or two opinions now has many. This is because knowledge is rare and desires are rampant. The result of this is that there is much division and confusion and very little unity.

From among the *tābiʿūn* are those who studied the whole of the Qur'ān from the companions. Mujāhid[13] said: "I read the whole Qur'ān to Ibn ʿAbbās[14] stopping him at the end of every verse, asking him concerning it." This is why al-Thawrī[15] would say: "If you read the exegesis of Mujāhid then that is sufficient for you." For this reason, scholars such as al-Shāfiʿī,[16] Bukhārī[17] and Imam Aḥmad[18] would heavily rely upon his narrations.

The point here is that the *tābiʿūn* studied the exegesis of the Qur'ān from the companions just as they took from them the Prophetic *Sunnah*. They would also comment on the Qur'ān using their deductions basing them on other evidences just as they did with the *ḥadīths* of the Prophet (ﷺ).

The students of the companions would increase in their commentary and deductions, more so than the companions. The reason for this being the occurrence of new matters which were not present during the time of the Prophet (ﷺ).

---

[13] Mujāhid ibn Jabr al-Makkī, died 104 AH. He was the most eminent student of the great commentator of the Qur'ān, Ibn ʿAbbās.

[14] ʿAbdullāh ibn ʿAbbās, died 68 AH. He was one of the most eminent scholars of the Qur'ān amongst the companions, known as the commentator of the Qur'ān. He is also the fourth most prolific narrator of *ḥadīth*.

[15] Abū ʿAbdullāh Sufyān ibn Masrūq al-Thawrī, died 161 AH. He was known as *amīr al-mu'minīn fil-ḥadīth* [leader of the faithful in *ḥadīth*]. He was born and brought up in Kūfah and refused the post of judge offered to him by Manṣūr and thereafter lived in Makkah and Madinah.

[16] Muḥammad ibn Idrīs al-Shāfiʿī, one of the four founders of the schools of *fiqh*, died 204 AH. He was born in Syria, raised in Makkah and went to study under Imām Mālik in Madinah. He later settled in Egypt.

[17] Muḥammad ibn Ismāʿīl ibn Ibrāhīm al-Bukhārī, died 256 AH, is the most outstanding compiler of *ḥadīth*. His famous work known as *Ṣaḥīḥ al-Bukhārī* is the most authentic collection of *ḥadīth*.

[18] Aḥmad ibn Muḥammad ibn Ḥanbal, died 241 AH. He was born in Marwa and raised in Baghdad. He is famously known for his legal school, his collection of *ḥadīth* and his defense of the views of the *salaf* on issues of faith.

Therefore, whenever something new arose and there was no clear text regarding it, the scholars of that time would have to deduce its ruling based upon the Qur'ān and *Sunnah*, for neither of these sources discusses every particular event which will take place until the Day of Judgement. Discussing every such event would have caused the Qur'ān to be a hundred times its current size. Furthermore, it would have discussed affairs which were yet to take place, such as cheques, banks, insurance policies etc. which would have caused confusion for earlier generations. Rather, whenever a new matter arises the scholars are able to deduce its rulings based upon the general principles of the Qur'ān and *Sunnah*.

Chapter 3

Differences of Opinion amongst the Predecessors in the Exegesis of the Qur'ān: A Difference of Variation

The predecessors differed little in the exegesis of the Qur'ān, however they differed considerably more in issues related to rulings (*aḥkām*). Whenever they do differ in the exegesis of the Qur'ān it is more a difference of variation than contradiction. This is of two categories:

Here the author asserts that differences amongst the predecessors in the exegesis of the Qur'ān may occur, but it is significantly less than their differences in rulings. The reason for this is that exegesis revolves around explaining words, their meanings and what is intended by them, and this is something in which there is not much difference. In contrast to this, rulings are based upon deduction and analogy, so differences are considerably more so than in *tafsīr*, due to a contrast in the levels of knowledge and understanding.

We have previously mentioned the difference between the explanation of the words of the Qur'ān and their meanings, and the fact that they are not necessarily one and the same. Explanation of the words is done by using other words to clarify the meaning of that particular word, whereas explanation of the meanings refers to the intended purpose behind those words depending upon the context and other such things.

The distinction between a difference of variation and a difference of contradiction is that in the latter one is unable to reconcile between the two sayings, for two contradictory saying cannot be reconciled. On the other hand, in a difference of variation one is able to reconcile the two sayings, for each saying mentions a different type, but both types belong to the same category, and as such, they are not contradictory. The author will now give some examples highlighting this.

The first: The expression of one and the same idea by using different words, such as them referring to the same concept by one mentioning a particular aspect concerning it and the other mentioning another aspect. These explanations are like using equivalent names which lie between synonyms and antonyms.

The author categorises a difference in variation into two:

The First Category: This is when the predecessors discuss the same concept but use alternative wordings. So each one alludes to a particular aspect of that word and expounds upon it, whilst still speaking about one and the same concept. An example of this is that one refers to a sword as being made of fine steel (*muhind*); another describes it as sharp (*ṣārim*), and a third as something which cuts and maims. In reality, this is not a difference as all are referring to the sword.

Another example is if one says a *ghaḍanfar* is a lion; a second says it is a large cat and a third describes it as a predatory animal. This is what the author means by his statement: The expression of one and the same idea by using different words, such as them referring to the same concept by one mentioning a particular aspect concerning it and the other mentioning another aspect.

These explanations are like using equivalent names which lie between synonyms and antonyms. This is a slightly ambiguous statement but I think he is referring to something else. Synonyms have a similar meaning, whereas antonyms have separate meanings. So these alternative words are similar as they refer to the same concept and idea, but separate in that they each use a different method in explaining that concept or word.

For example, it is said whilst mentioning alternative names for 'sword': '*ṣārim*' and '*muhind*'. Similar to this are the names of Allāh, the names of the Prophet (ﷺ) and the names of the Qur'ān. The names of Allāh all refer to Him, the Most High.

The names of Allāh, the Most High, are many in number but they all refer to the same being. They are synonymous as they all refer to Allāh, and are different in that they refer to Him by using a particular attribute which also possesses a certain meaning. Similar to this are the names of the Messenger (ﷺ). Likewise, the Qur'ān is also referred to as the 'Criterion' and the 'Divine Revelation', but all these names even though they are different in their words refer to the same thing.

Therefore, supplicating to Him using one of His names is not contradictory to supplicating to Him using another name. Rather, it is as Allāh has mentioned:

قُلِ ٱدْعُوا۟ ٱللَّهَ أَوِ ٱدْعُوا۟ ٱلرَّحْمَٰنَ ۖ أَيًّا مَّا تَدْعُوا۟ فَلَهُ ٱلْأَسْمَآءُ ٱلْحُسْنَىٰ ۚ

Say, "Call upon Allāh or call upon the Most Merciful [al-Raḥmān]. Whichever [name] you call – to Him belong the best names."

Sūrah al-Isrā', 17:110

Each of His names refers to Allāh Himself as well as the attribute which that name possesses. For example, the All-Knowing refers to Allāh and the attribute of knowledge. The All-Powerful refers to Allāh and the attribute of power. The Most Merciful refers to Allāh and the attribute of mercy.

These three names mentioned here as examples are synonymous as they all refer to Allāh. At the same time, they differ in the sense that one refers to knowledge, the second to power and the third to the mercy of Allāh.

Whosoever rejects that these names point to attributes are from those who claim to only accept the apparent [i.e. literalists]. They have made a claim similar to the extreme *Bāṭiniyyah Qarāmiṭah* who state: 'It is not said that He is living or not living.' They negate both opposites. This group does not reject words such as pronouns; they only deny the attributes which these names possess. Whosoever agrees with their extreme views in this respect has conformed to the way of the *Bāṭiniyyah*, and this is not the place to expand upon this topic.

Due to the authors great expertise in this field, he has mentioned this point.

Regarding the names of Allāh, people are divided into three groups. The first group has made them simply names, void of any meanings. The second group has affirmed the names and the attributes they possess. The third group claims: 'We do not state that He is living nor that He is not living, so we reject both.' This group is the *Bāṭiniyyah*. Their argument is that life and death cannot be affirmed or negated except for the one that it is applicable to, and this is not applicable to Allāh. Similarly, a wall is not described as being dead or alive.

In response to this argument we say: This claim that life and death can only be ascribed to one that it is applicable to is futile, for Allāh describes idols as being dead, and not living:

وَالَّذِينَ يَدْعُونَ مِن دُونِ اللَّهِ لَا يَخْلُقُونَ شَيْئًا وَهُمْ يُخْلَقُونَ ﴿٢٠﴾ أَمْوَاتٌ غَيْرُ أَحْيَاءٍ

And those they invoke other than Allāh create nothing, and they [themselves] are created. They are, [in fact], dead.

Sūrah al-Naḥl, 16:19-20

They used to worship objects such as trees and stones. Hence, the Qur'ān has refuted this statement of theirs.

As for their argument: 'If we say Allāh is alive we compare Him to the living, and if we say He is dead we compare Him to the dead.' We respond by saying that instead you have compared Him to inanimate objects such as stones.

Furthermore, even if for the sake of argument we were to accept this, you further state that Allāh is neither existent nor non-existent. Denying both of these aspects is something which leads to the impossible which no intellectual person will accept, for such a claim leads to denying both opposites. If one is lifted then the other must be present. Also, to claim that to describe Allāh as existent or non-existent is atheism makes no sense, for this instead leads to Him being something which is imaginary. This is the belief of the *Bāṭiniyyah*.

The first of these three groups are the *Muʿtazilah* and the literalists who affirm the names without any meaning. They say that He is All-Hearing without hearing, All-Knowing without knowledge, Merciful without mercy and so on. This is similar to the one who is called Muḥammad [literally the praiseworthy one] but he possesses no praiseworthy characteristics or ʿAbdullāh [the slave of Allāh] even though he disbelieves in Him. Hence these names simply point out those people who possess these names. They claim that the names of Allāh are similar to this.

This last paragraph mentioned by the author is not relevant to the topic at hand. The only significance is that the names of Allāh are mentioned many times throughout the Qur'ān.

The point being that every single name of Allāh refers to Him and the attributes that name possesses. By necessity, it also refers to the attributes which other names may possess.

Each name refers to the attributes it possesses as well as other attributes which can be derived from other names by necessity. For example, the name 'the Creator' refers to Allāh and the attribute of creating. By necessity it also implies the attribute of knowledge present in the name 'the All-Knowing' and power which is present in the name 'the All-Powerful.' The 'Creator' implies both the attribute of knowledge and power because one cannot create without possessing knowledge, power and ability. This is why Allāh states:

ٱللَّهُ ٱلَّذِى خَلَقَ
سَبْعَ سَمَٰوَٰتٍ وَمِنَ ٱلْأَرْضِ مِثْلَهُنَّ يَتَنَزَّلُ ٱلْأَمْرُ بَيْنَهُنَّ لِتَعْلَمُوٓا۟ أَنَّ
ٱللَّهَ عَلَىٰ كُلِّ شَىْءٍ قَدِيرٌ وَأَنَّ ٱللَّهَ قَدْ أَحَاطَ بِكُلِّ شَىْءٍ عِلْمًۢا ﴿١٢﴾

It is Allāh who has created seven heavens and of the earth, the like of them. [His] command descends among them so you may know that Allāh is over all things competent and that Allāh has encompassed all things in knowledge.

Surah al-Ṭalāq, 65:12

This is something well known and accepted, for if someone wanted to construct a device he would not be able to do so unless he possessed the relevant knowledge and had the necessary physical ability.

Similar to this are the names of the Prophet (ﷺ) such as: Muḥammad, Aḥmad, *al-Māḥiy* [the one who extinguishes], *al-Ḥāshir* [the one who gathers] and *al-'Āqib* [the last prophet]. Likewise, the names of the Qur'ān include: *al-Furqān* [the criterion], *al-Hudā* [the guide], *al-Shifā'* [the cure], *al-Bayān* [the clarification] and *al-Kitāb* [the Book].

If the intention of the questioner is to pinpoint an object, it can be described by using any name so long as it is understood to refer to that particular object. This description may be in the form of a noun or an attribute. For example, the one who asks concerning the verse:

وَمَنْ أَعْرَضَ عَن ذِكْرِي

And whosoever turns away from My remembrance
Sūrah Ṭā-Hā, 20:124

What is the remembrance? The answer is: 'It is the Qur'ān' or 'It is His divinely revealed Books.' The word remembrance is a noun, and a noun is either attached to the subject [the one who remembers] or the object [what is being remembered]. Therefore, the remembrance of Allāh in relation to the second meaning is like the statement: *Subḥān Allāh* [All glory be to Allāh], *Alḥamdulillāh* [All praise is for Allāh], *Lā ilāha illallāh* [none has the right to be worshipped but Allāh] and *Allāhu Akbar* [Allāh is the greatest]. In relation to the first meaning [i.e. the subject] it refers to the one who is remembering His speech, and this is what is being referred to in this verse.

This is further supported by the verse which precedes this verse:

فَإِمَّا يَأْتِيَنَّكُم مِّنِّي هُدًى فَمَنِ اتَّبَعَ هُدَايَ فَلَا يَضِلُّ
وَلَا يَشْقَىٰ ﴿١٢٣﴾

And if there should come to you guidance from Me – then whoever follows My guidance will neither go astray [in the world] nor suffer [in the Hereafter].

Sūrah Ṭā-Hā, 20:123

His guidance is that which He has revealed. Allāh then states:

قَالَ رَبِّ لِمَ حَشَرْتَنِىٓ أَعْمَىٰ وَقَدْ كُنتُ بَصِيرًا ﴿١٢٥﴾

قَالَ كَذَٰلِكَ أَتَتْكَ ءَايَٰتُنَا فَنَسِيتَهَا

He will say, "My Lord, why have you raised me blind while I was [once] seeing?" [Allāh] will say, "Thus did Our signs come to you, and you forgot [i.e. disregarded] them; and thus will you this Day be forgotten."

Sūrah Ṭā-Hā, 20:125-126

The point being that what is intended by the remembrance is His revealed speech or the remembrance of that speech by the servant. Therefore, whether it is said: 'My remembrance' means 'My Book' or 'My speech' or 'My guidance', the intended meaning is one and the same.

Here, the author (may Allāh have mercy upon him) is saying: If the questioner – who is asking concerning the exegesis of a particular verse – wishes to refer to something, he may refer to it using any name so long as that name is known to represent what he is describing. For example, if one were to ask: What does the following verse mean: ***"And whosoever turns away from My remembrance"?*** Does this mean whosoever turns away from the remembrance of Allāh or whosoever turns away from the remembrance which I revealed?

The answer to this question is that it can refer to both. It can refer to the remembrance of Allāh, as Allāh says:

وَأَقِمِ ٱلصَّلَوٰةَ لِذِكۡرِيٓ ١٤

And establish the prayer for My remembrance
Sūrah Ṭā-Hā, 20:14

i.e. so that you may remember Me via the prayer. Similarly, the verse can be referring to the remembrance Allāh revealed which is the Qur'ān. The latter of the two meanings is stronger considering the context. Allāh states in the previous verse: ***"And if there should come to you guidance from Me – then whoever follows My guidance will neither go astray [in the world] nor suffer [in the Hereafter]"***. The guidance in this verse refers to the revelation. ***"And whosoever turns away from My remembrance"***. The reason as to why it is called guidance in the former verse and remembrance in the latter is because this guidance which He revealed contains a reminder and a warning for mankind.

If in this previous example one asked about the meaning of the word 'remembrance' and was told it means saying *Subḥān Allāh* (All glory be to Allāh), *Alḥamdulillāh* (All praise is for Allāh) and *Allāhu Akbar* (Allāh is the greatest) then this is a correct explanation. Likewise if one said the word 'remembrance' refers to that which Allāh has revealed from the Books then this is also a correct explanation, for the word 'remembrance' correctly signifies both meanings. This is what a difference of expression is. The first interpretation does not contradict the second as that which Allāh revealed necessitates His remembrance.

However, if the intention of the questioner is to learn about the attribute which that name also connotes, then an added explanation must also be given. For example, it is possible for one to ask concerning the names of Allāh: *al-Quddūs* (the Pure), *al-Salām* (the Perfect), *al-Mu'min* (the Bestower of Faith) even though one knows that these names refer to Allāh but he wishes to inquire about these specific attributes.

If one were to ask: 'Who is *al-Quddūs*?' The response would be: 'Allāh.' This differs however, from the one who asks: 'What does *al-Quddūs* mean?' In response to this question one must explain the meaning of this word.

If that which has preceded is clear, one realises that it is often the case that the predecessors (*salaf*) would describe something using a name which points to the object being referred to; at the same time this name may also contain an attribute not present in its other names. Just as the Prophet (ﷺ) is described as: *al-Ḥāshir*, *al-Māḥiy* and *al-ʿĀqib*, and Allāh is *al-Ghafūr* and *al-Raḥīm*. All these names refer to one and the same thing but each also contains a unique attribute.

This is a possible third answer to the question: Who is *al-Quddūs*? The response is that He is the Knower of the witnessed and the unseen, or He is the One whose mercy envelopes all things, or He is the Oft-Forgiving, Most Merciful. In this answer it is understood that I am referring to Allāh, but it is done by mentioning a name which contains an attribute not present in the name being asked about.

Therefore, if the questioner asks: Who is *al-Quddūs*? one may respond by saying that 'He is severe in punishment to those who disobey Him', wishing to emphasise this attribute in order to remind the questioner of this aspect as he happens to be a person indulging in sin. On the other hand if a person is in a weak and fearful state, the answer to the previous question posed can be: 'He is as His servant thinks of Him', in order to encourage that person to think good of Allāh.

In conclusion then there are three types which we have discussed: The first being an explanation of what is intended by that word. The second type is the meaning that it comprises. The third type is to use another name which mentions a different attribute.

It is well-known that this is not a difference of contradiction as some people mistakenly think. For example, what does the 'straight path' refer to? Some scholars mention it is to follow the Qur'ān due to the statement of the Prophet (ﷺ), *"The Qur'ān is the firm rope of Allāh, the wise reminder and the straight path."*[19] Others have stated that the straight path refers to Islām due to the *ḥadīth* of the Prophet (ﷺ) narrated by al-Nawwās ibn Sam'ān:

"Allāh has set forth the parable of a straight path; on either side of this path there is a wall in which there are open doors and upon these doors are curtains. There is a man calling from the top of the road and another from above the road. He said: The straight path is Islām. The walls are the boundaries of Allāh. The open doors are the prohibitions. The caller from the top of the road is the Book of Allāh, and the caller from above the road is the admonisher from Allāh which every believer hears in his heart."[20]

So both of the explanations mentioned for the 'straight path' are in reality the same, as the religion of Islām is to follow the Qur'ān. However each description points to a particular aspect not present in the other description. The word 'path' also signifies a third meaning. Similar to this are all the other explanations given for the 'straight path', that it is *al-Sunnah wal Jamā'ah*, or the path of worship, or it is obedience to Allāh and His Messenger (ﷺ). All of these explanations refer to one and the same thing; however each one chooses to describe it using a particular attribute.

We have already mentioned that if some of the *salaf* explain a word by one meaning and others explain it by another meaning, and that word comprises both meanings then this is a difference in expression. Therefore in the verse ***"Guide us to the straight path"***, a path linguistically is a large way. In this verse it is

[19] *Sunan al-Tirmidhī*, no. 2906.

[20] Ibid, no. 2859.

explained as being Islām or the Qur'ān, the author supported each of the two sayings with evidence from the *Sunnah*. Both of the sayings are not contradictory as Islām is what is in the Qur'ān. As such, this is a difference in expression as each of the sayings does not oppose or negate the other.

The second category:[21] To mention by way of example and illustration some aspects of the general term being referred to, in order to draw the attention of the listener to the type of thing that is being referred to and not to completely define the boundaries of the word. Thus, if a non-Arab asked about the word *khubz* (bread) and was shown a *raghīf* (a loaf of bread), this illustrates to that person that similar things are known as *khubz*, not that this particular loaf alone can be described as such.

In this example a non-Arab asks: 'What is *khubz*?' If one were to reply: '*Khubz* is something round in shape, made from wheat which is grounded and mixed with water and then made into dough,' such an explanation would not be sufficient. However, if you were to show a person a piece of bread then he would not believe that this was the only bread available in the whole world, but he would understand that this is an example of what is being referred to. Furthermore, he would then be able to go to a shop and buy some bread. Thus, this description of bread is not meant to be an absolute definition which cannot be changed, but just an example.

[21] i.e. the second of the two categories in the difference of variation.

An example of this is the Qur'ānic verse:

ثُمَّ أَوْرَثْنَا ٱلْكِتَٰبَ ٱلَّذِينَ ٱصْطَفَيْنَا مِنْ عِبَادِنَا ۖ
فَمِنْهُمْ ظَالِمٌ لِّنَفْسِهِۦ وَمِنْهُم مُّقْتَصِدٌ وَمِنْهُمْ
سَابِقٌۢ بِٱلْخَيْرَٰتِ بِإِذْنِ ٱللَّهِ ۚ

Then We caused to inherit the Book those We have chosen of Our servants, and among them is he who wrongs himself [i.e. sins], and among them is he who is moderate, and among them is he who is foremost in good deeds by the permission of Allāh.

Sūrah Fāṭir, 35:32

Those who have been chosen by Allāh refers to the Muslims, for the last Book which was revealed was this Qur'ān.

Those who wrong themselves are those who do not perform the obligatory duties and embark upon that which has been prohibited. The moderate are those who fulfil their obligations and refrain from prohibitions. Those who are foremost are the ones who not only do that which is obligated upon them but perform optional acts too. Thus, the moderate will be the people on the right, and the foremost will be the foremost; those who are brought near [to Allāh].

Furthermore, each one of these three can be described by the way in which they perform a certain act. It can be said that the foremost are those who pray their daily prayers at their proper time, the moderate are those who pray within the allotted duration, and those who wrong themselves are those who delay the prayer until the time is about to pass. Likewise it can be said that these three types of people are also mentioned in *Sūrah al-Baqarah*, the good-doer is mentioned as being charitable, the wrong-doer deals in usury and the just busies himself in trade, so with regards to wealth people are generous, just or oppressive. Thus, the foremost are those who are generous by not only fulfilling the obligatory act but also giving extra. The oppressive are those who deal in usury or refuse to pay the *Zakāh*, and the moderate are those who give *Zakāh* but do not deal in usury.

Therefore, each saying mentions something which is already present in the verse; it is merely stressed in order to draw attention to that particular aspect of the verse by way of example. For defining something by way of illustration or example can be much easier than defining something with an absolute definition.

It is the case that examples better clarify the intended meaning of something, more so than the actual definition. If for example you were asked: What is a camel? And you were to reply: It is a large bodied animal, possessing a long neck, humps and a short tail; a person may still be ambiguous regarding the camel. Even if he was then to pass by one he would still doubt whether or not it was actually a camel, as other animals may be similar to it. If on the other hand, he was given an example of what the camel looked like, it would instantly become clear.

For this reason, many scholars of *fiqh* (jurisprudence) – may Allāh have mercy upon them – define terms with their rulings. For instance they say, an obligatory act is that which causes the doer to be rewarded, and the one who leaves it is entitled to punishment. This is clearer than stating an obligatory act is that which the *sharīʿah* has ordered by necessity.

The point being that the *salaf* explained the verse mentioned by the author by saying that the one who oppresses himself is he who delays the prayer beyond its time. The moderate one is he who prays it within its allotted duration and the foremost are those who pray it at its earliest time, or to be more precise its proper time, so as to include those prayers which it is better to delay such as *ʿIshā'*.

Someone else could explain the above verse with another act such as *Zakāh*. The formeost are those who give *Zakāh* as well as optional charity. The moderate are those who just give the obligatory *Zakāh*, and the oppressive are those who don't give the *Zakāh*. These two explanations of the above verse are not contradictory, for each one mentions something which the verse implies, even though the verse is much more general and includes all in which one can be moderate, foremost or oppressive.

One's intellect can easily relate to an example of something, just as it understands what bread is when it is shown a loaf. From this category is also the statement: The reason this verse was revealed was due to such and such, especially if it was due to a person. This is the case with the background regarding the revelation of certain verses.

For example, they state that the verse concerning *ẓihār*[22] was revealed concerning the wife of Aws ibn al-Ṣāmit. The verse of *liʿān*[23] was revealed concerning ʿUwaymir al-ʿAjlānī or Hilāl ibn Umayyah, and the verse of *kalālah*[24] was revealed in the case of Jābir ibn ʿAbdullāh. Similarly, the verse:

وَأَنِ ٱحْكُم بَيْنَهُم بِمَآ أَنزَلَ ٱللَّهُ

And judge, [O Muḥammad], between them by what Allāh has revealed

Sūrah al-Mā'idah, 5:49

was revealed during the incident of *Banū Qurayẓah* and *Banū Naḍīr*. The verse:

وَمَن يُوَلِّهِمْ يَوْمَئِذٍ دُبُرَهُۥٓ

And whoever turns his back to them on such a day

Sūrah al-Anfāl, 8:16

was revealed concerning [the battle of] *Badr*. Likewise, the verse:

شَهَٰدَةُ بَيْنِكُمْ إِذَا حَضَرَ أَحَدَكُمُ ٱلْمَوْتُ

[22] Translator's note: See Sūrah al-Mujādilah, 58:1-4.

[23] Translator's note: See Sūrah al-Nūr, 24:6-9.

[24] Translator's note: See Sūrah al-Nisā', 4:176.

...testimony [should be taken] among you when death approaches one of you
Sūrah al-Mā'idah, 5:106

was revealed in the story of Tamīm al-Dārī and 'Adiyy ibn Badā'. Also, the statement of Abū Ayyūb about the verse:

وَلَا تُلْقُوا۟ بِأَيْدِيكُمْ إِلَى ٱلتَّهْلُكَةِ

...and do not throw [yourselves] with your [own] hands into destruction
Sūrah al-Baqarah, 2:195

'It was revealed concerning us: the *Anṣār*.' There are many such examples where it is mentioned that a certain verse was revealed concerning the polytheists of Makkah or the Jews and Christians, or concerning a group of believers. The purpose of such statements is not to insinuate that these verses only pertained to these people and no one else; this would not be said by a Muslim or an intelligent person.

The only point of difference is concerning a general term which is used in a particular case; is it limited to that case or not? None of the Muslim scholars infer that the general terms present in the Qur'ān and *Sunnah* only pertain to those specific people about whom those verses were revealed. Rather, the most that can be said is that such said verses apply to all those who are similar to that person for which the verse was revealed, and the wording is not generalised to the limits to which the language allows.

This saying is the correct opinion, i.e. that it includes all those who are in a similar position to that person about whom the verse was revealed. An example of this is the saying of the Prophet (ﷺ): *"It is not from piety to fast while travelling."*[25] The wording of

[25] Sahih al-Bukhāri, no. 1946, and Sahih Muslim, no. 1115.

this *ḥadīth* is general; however it is specific to this situation and to such a person.

Does this then mean that it was only relevant to that specific person about whom the *ḥadīth* is discussing? The author states that this is not claimed by any of the Muslims. Does it mean that it is specific to that type of person; one who finds himself in a similar situation? This is possible if we know the exact circumstances which surrounded the incident.

Therefore, if we take the general wording of this *ḥadīth* the meaning is: It is not from piety to fast while travelling, irrespective of whether or not fasting will cause hardship. If we were to specify this *ḥadīth* to a particular person, then the meaning is that it is not from piety for that specific person to fast. This is also a wrong interpretation as the author mentions. The third possibility is to state that it is not from piety to fast for a person who finds himself in a similar situation to the one in the *ḥadīth*, i.e. he finds hardship and difficulty in fasting. This third saying is the middle ground and the correct opinion.

The point being made is that to search for the reason and to use that as the basis for deducing the ruling is better than to simply generalise. There is a difference between saying "It is not from piety," and saying, "Piety is not to fast." The former statement implies that what is not from piety is from sin. However, if someone does not wish to take the *rukhṣah* [legal permission] then he is not sinful, except if he believes he is not in need of the ease which Allāh has allowed him to take. If on the other hand he acknowledges this easy route and thanks Allāh for it but prefers to fast then that is another matter.

Any verse which was revealed for a particular reason, especially if the verse is an order or a prohibition, not only includes that particular person for whom it was revealed but all those similar to him. This is also the case if the verse is praising or censuring someone.

Knowledge of the reasons for which a verse was revealed assists one in understanding that verse, for knowledge of the cause helps to bring about knowledge of the result. For this reason, the stronger of the two opinions concerning a person who forgets the oath he took is that one returns to the reason which caused him to take the oath in the first place. What caused it and what factors led to it?

Similarly, if the intention of the one who divorced is not known then we return to the reason which led him to divorce. For example, if a man saw another man with his wife and divorced her because of that, then later realised that it was her brother then the divorce does not count. It was as if he was saying I am divorcing you because you were with a foreign man.

Likewise, if one takes an oath by Allāh that he will not visit someone, because he has been told that so and so is a sinner, and then he later finds out that he is not, then he can visit him and no expiation is due. The reason for this is that it is as if the person placed a condition on his oath, i.e. I will not visit so and so as long as he is a sinner, and when it becomes clear that he is not a sinner he may visit him as the condition is like a clause. This is a general principle which can be used in oaths and divorces. However this differs from the one who says: 'I swear by Allāh I will never visit so and so for any reason whatsoever,' because here the person has made his intention quite clear. If he was to then go and visit that person he would have broken his oath. Thus, the rule is: every word which is based upon a reason and then that reason is removed is void.

In what the author is discussing, the verse or the *ḥadīth* is the result. For example, the reason why the verse of *liʿān* was revealed was due to Hilāl ibn Umayyah accusing his wife of having relations with Shurayk ibn Saḥmā', so this was the reason and the result was that certain verses were revealed concerning this. So the meaning of a verse or *ḥadīth* can remain hidden until we know the background and the reason behind it.

Their statement: 'This verse was revealed due to such and such' can sometimes mean that this was the reason the verse was revealed.

The author often digresses in his books. Here, he has digressed in order to mention the different expressions used when discussing the reasons for revelation (*asbāb al-nuzūl*). They are of three types:

The first expression is: 'Such and such happened, so the following verse was revealed.' The second expression which may be used: 'The reason such and such verse was revealed was because of such and such.' The third: 'The verse was revealed due to such and such.'

The second of the three expressions is explicit in mentioning the reason. The first expression is also apparent in its reference to the reason of revelation even if it is not explicit. The third expression is probable; it can either be referring to the meaning of the verse or to the reason of revelation.

Hence, the three types of expressions which are used to describe the reason for the revelation of a verse can be classed as: explicit, apparent and probable.

It can also imply that this meaning is also present in the verse even if it is not the reason for its revelation, i.e. the meaning of this verse is such and such. The scholars have differed regarding the statement of a companion: 'This verse was revealed due to such and such.' Does this statement count as being a prophetic narration just as if the companion was to narrate the incident as it took place, or is it considered an explanation which the companion gives himself and not a [prophetic] narration? Al-Bukhārī considered it to be a narration whereas others did not. The majority of books containing narrations fall into the latter category such as *Musnad Aḥmad*. If on the other hand, the companion describes the incident as a narration then all agree that it is a narration.

If this statement of the companion is considered to be a narration this suggests it took place during the time of the Prophet (ﷺ), so the verse was revealed in order to explain an incident and its rulings. If we don't consider it to be a narration then it becomes his explanation (*tafsīr*) of the verse, and as such it may be correct or others may oppose his views.

If this is known and one states: 'This verse was revealed due to this,' this does not contradict a similar statement from someone else, so long as the word can include both meanings as we have explained when discussing *tafsīr* by way of example. Likewise, if one mentions a reason for which the verse was revealed and then another mentions a different reason, it is possible that both are speaking the truth and that the verse was revealed after a number of incidents took place, or the verse was revealed twice, on each occasion for a different reason.

The first reason is more likely. If more than one person mentions a reason for the revelation of a verse either explicitly or apparently as has been previously stated, does this mean that the reasons are different but the result [i.e. the verse] is one? Or is it possible that the reasons are multiple and the result is also multiple, and that the verse was revealed for two separate reasons? The first is more likely, for a verse to be revealed more than once is against the norm. Thus all reasons and incidents took place before this as it is possible that a number of incidents preceded the revelation of a verse. It is also rare, if not incorrect for one verse to be revealed more than once. However, it is mentioned that *Sūrah al-Fātihah* was revealed once in Makkah and then again in Madīnah, and Allāh knows best.

The point being stressed here is that if there is more than one reason which explicitly states the background of a verse then it can mean one of two things: Firstly that the reasons are multiple and one verse was revealed, or the reasons were multiple and so was the revelation of the verse. This is only if both statements are explicit. However, if one is apparent and the other is probable, then we obviously give precedence to the apparent statement. Likewise, if one statement is explicit and another apparent, priority is given to the explicit. In such a case, the explicit statement is taken as being the reason for revelation and the apparent statement is considered to be referring to the meaning of the verse. An example of this can be given in the verse:

فَوَيۡلٞ لِّلۡمُصَلِّينَ ٤ ٱلَّذِينَ هُمۡ عَن صَلَاتِهِمۡ سَاهُونَ

So woe to those who pray. [But] who are heedless of their prayer

Sūrah al-Māʿūn, 107:4-5

It can be said that this verse was revealed concerning those who delay the prayer beyond its time. This statement does not mean that delaying the prayer was the reason for its revelation but that it is what the verse is referring to. Hence, such a statement is an explanation of the verse.

These two different categories of tafsīr which we have just mentioned – variation in names and attributes or different categories and types with which they are described such as illustrations – are the two most predominant types of *tafsīr* found among the predecessors which may be thought of as differences in opinion.

An example of difference in names and attributes are the different names which can be given to a sword as previously mentioned. Difference in illustration and example can be taken from the verse: ***"and among them is he who wrongs himself [i.e. sins], and among them is he who is moderate, and among them is he who is foremost in good deeds,"*** where the example has been given of the prayer and charity.

Another type of difference which can be found is where we have ambiguous words. This can be done in two ways. Firstly, it is ambiguous because it has a number of meanings in the language such as the word '*qaswarah*' which can refer to a shooter or a lion, and the word "*as'asa*' which can refer to both the advent and departure of the night.

An ambiguous word is a single word which possesses a number of meanings, such as the word '*qaswarah*' which can refer to a shooter or a lion. Allāh states:

﴿٤٩﴾ كَأَنَّهُمْ حُمُرٌ مُّسْتَنفِرَةٌ ﴿٥٠﴾ فَرَّتْ مِن قَسْوَرَةٍ ﴿٥١﴾

As if they were alarmed donkeys. Fleeing from a lion.
Sūrah al-Muddaththir, 74:50-51

Wild donkeys flee from hunters and domestic donkeys flee from predators such as lions. Thus, some scholars have stated this word refers to a hunter whilst others say it refers to a lion, and so long as the word implies both meanings without contradiction, there is no harm in applying both meanings.

Likewise in the verse:

وَالَّيْلِ إِذَا عَسْعَسَ ﴿١٧﴾ وَالصُّبْحِ إِذَا تَنَفَّسَ ﴿١٨﴾

And by the night as it closes in. And by the dawn when it breathes.
Sūrah al-Takwīr, 81:17-18

Again here some scholars have said that "*as'asa*' is the beginning of the night whilst others have said it is the end of the night. Thus, the word carries both meanings unless there is an indication to show that one meaning is preferred over the other in this context. Therefore, either Allāh is taking an oath by the beginning and end of the night in this verse, or just by the beginning. If we take into consideration the next verse which shows the contrast as it mentions the dawn which is the end of the night, this indicates that the more appropriate meaning in this context is the beginning of the night. Another example of an ambiguous word which is used in the Qur'ān is '*qar*" which can refer to the monthly cycle of a woman or the state of purity which follows the end of such a cycle.

[The second way it can be ambiguous] is because even though the word originally only has one meaning, it denotes one of two different types or one of two things such as a pronominal subject which at times can refer to a number of things, like in the verse:

ثُمَّ دَنَا فَتَدَلَّىٰ ﴿٨﴾ فَكَانَ قَابَ قَوْسَيْنِ أَوْ أَدْنَىٰ ﴿٩﴾

Then he approached and descended. And was at a distance of two bow lengths or nearer

Sūrah al-Najm, 53:8-9

Allāh says:

ذُو مِرَّةٍ فَاسْتَوَىٰ ﴿٦﴾ وَهُوَ بِالْأُفُقِ الْأَعْلَىٰ ﴿٧﴾ ثُمَّ دَنَا فَتَدَلَّىٰ ﴿٨﴾
فَكَانَ قَابَ قَوْسَيْنِ أَوْ أَدْنَىٰ ﴿٩﴾ فَأَوْحَىٰ إِلَىٰ عَبْدِهِ مَا أَوْحَىٰ ﴿١٠﴾

One of soundness. And he rose to [his] true form. While he was in the higher [part of the] horizon. Then he approached and descended. And was at a distance of two bow lengths or nearer. And He revealed to His servant what He revealed.

Sūrah al-Najm, 53:6-10

The pronominal subject in 'Then he approached' refers to Jibril, whereas in the last verse mentioned [He] refers to Allāh. This is the most correct opinion.[26]

[26] Translator's Note: Here Shaykh Ibn 'Uthaymīn is mentioning one of the opinions regarding the explanation of these verses. The point being stressed here is that the pronominal subject in both verses is 'he', but in one it refers to the angel Jibrīl and in the other it refers to Allāh. This shows how one word can refer to two things. For this reason the scholars may differ over the explanation of a verse due to the presence of such similar words.

Other similar words include: *al-fajr* (the day-break), *al-shafʿ* (the even), *al-watr* (the odd) and *layālin ʿashar* (the ten nights). It is possible that these words have the meanings the salaf gave to them, or their meanings could be otherwise.

The first is the case when a verse is revealed twice, once for one reason and then again due to another reason, or because of an ambiguous word where both meanings can be correctly applied. This is the opinion of the majority of the scholars of the Mālikī, Shāfiʿī and Ḥanbalī schools of thought as well as many theologians. The other case is where one word has only one meaning making it general so long as there is nothing which specifies its meaning. If both meanings are permitted then this will fall into the second category.

The author is discussing another type of difference which is present; that is when one word can have two possible meanings. He then mentions that such a word is due to one of two reasons:

Firstly: When the word has multiple meanings, such as the word '*ʿayn*'.

Secondly: When the word only has one meaning but can refer to one of two things. Such a word originally has one meaning, such as *insān* (human), *ḥajar* (rock), *shams* (sun), *qamar* (moon) etc. The author then mentions that such a word can refer to one of its two types. Even though this is rare, it is determined by the context in which the word is placed.

For example the word '*maʿa*' which literally means 'with' has only one meaning which denotes companionship, however this companionship can be of types depending upon the context in which it is found. If you were to say: 'Water with milk' this refers to a mixture, whereas: 'a wife with her husband' implies that it is a companionship of marriage, and if you were to say: 'a general with his troops' this refers to his leadership, not that he is constantly in their company. Thus, even though this word has one meaning which is companionship, the type of companionship can differ depending upon the context.

Similar to this are the pronominal subjects mentioned by the author. If there is a difference of opinion regarding what they are referring to, we say: If the word can correctly be upheld with both meanings then this is a difference in variation, otherwise it is a contradiction. The author also questions as to whether or not both meanings of an ambiguous word can be applied, i.e. both meanings used? The answer is that this is allowed so long as the two meanings do not negate one another. We have already given an example of this with the word '*qaswarah*' which can mean hunter or lion. There is no indication which gives one meaning preference over the other, and the two meanings do not negate each other. Therefore both can be correctly applied.

On the other hand, if there was a contradiction between the two meanings then it is not possible to apply them both. For example, the word '*qar*'' means menses or the state of purity which follows the menses. Since the two meanings cannot both be correctly applied as they each contradict the other and imply different rulings, both meanings cannot be correct.

Likewise, in the *ḥadīth*: "*Whosoever leaves [i.e. for the Jum'ah prayer] in the first hour...*"[27] The word '*rawāḥ*' can refer to leaving in general or leaving after midday. Since the two meanings cannot both be correctly applied in this *ḥadīth*, both cannot be used. One implies that you do not leave for the prayer until after midday soon after which the *imām* begins his sermon. The other meaning implies that one can leave at any time after sunrise.

The verses of *Sūrah al-Fajr* state: ***"By the dawn. And the ten nights."*** Some scholars say the ten nights refer to the last ten of Ramaḍān, while others insist they refer to the first ten of Dhul-Ḥijjah. Also, the next verse: ***"And [by] the even [number] and***

[27] *Muwaṭṭa Mālik*, vol. 1, p. 101.

the odd." Some say that the 'odd number' refers to Allāh, based upon the *ḥadīth*: *"Indeed, Allāh is an odd number [i.e. One]."*[28] The 'even number' refers to the creation due to the verse:

وَمِن كُلِّ شَيْءٍ خَلَقْنَا زَوْجَيْنِ لَعَلَّكُمْ تَذَكَّرُونَ ﴿٤٩﴾

And of all things We created two mates [i.e. counterparts]; perhaps you will remember.
Sūrah al-Dhāriyāt, 51:49

Other scholars state that the 'even and odd' refer to numbers, as all creation is either an odd or even number. In reality, both meanings can be correctly applied.

Likewise, prayer is also an odd number. The night prayer is concluded by the *witr* prayer [an odd number of *rakʿahs*] and the daylight prayers are also concluded by a *witr* (odd) prayer which is *Maghrib*. Thus, having prayers which have an even number of *rakʿahs* [such as *Ẓuhr* and *ʿAsr*] does not negate there being an odd numbered prayer such as *Maghrib*, as the Prophet (ﷺ) described it: *"It is the odd prayer of the day."*[29] The Prophet (ﷺ) also said: *"When one of you fears the morning is about to enter then let him pray one and it will be a witr for that which he has prayed."*[30] In conclusion, both meanings can be correctly applied to this verse as they do not contradict one another.

---

[28] *Sahih al-Bukhāri*, no. 6410, *Sahih Muslim*, no. 2677.

[29] *Sunan al-Tirmidhī*, no. 552.

[30] *Sahih al-Bukhāri*, no. 472, *Sahih Muslim*, no. 749.

Another statement of theirs which is commonly thought to be a difference of opinion, is when they express an opinion each using a different choice of words. These words are similar in their connotations but not synonymous. There are very few words in the Arabic language which are synonymous; this is even rarer in the Qur'ān if not non-existent. It is rare to express the exact same meaning using two sets of words; at best, the meanings will be approximate. This is from the miracles of the Qur'ān.

Here, the author states that there are very few synonyms in the Arabic language. A synonym is two words having the exact same meaning in every sense. This statement is correct as it relates to meanings. As for objects, then many objects possess names which are synonymous [i.e. they refer to the same object]. For example, there are many names for a lion and a cat. Even though this is rare when it comes to meanings it is still present and cannot be denied, as grain and wheat are synonymous.

In terms of the Qur'ān, there is no word which can be substituted for another. However some people believe that the word '*shakk*' in the verse:

فَإِن كُنتَ فِي شَكٍّ مِّمَّآ أَنزَلْنَآ إِلَيْكَ

So if you are in doubt, [O Muḥammad], about that which We have revealed to you

Sūrah Yūnus, 10:94

is exactly synonymous with the word '*rayb*' in the verse:

لَا رَيْبَ فِيهِ هُدًى لِّلْمُتَّقِينَ ﴿٢﴾

...about which there is no doubt, a guidance for those conscious of Allāh.

Sūrah al-Baqarah, 2:2

However this is not the case as will be mentioned by the author. Therefore, to have two words which are synonymous in every sense is rare or non-existent.

If one were to say regarding the verse:

يَوْمَ تَمُورُ ٱلسَّمَآءُ مَوْرًا ﴿٩﴾

On the Day the heaven will sway with the circular motion
Sūrah al-Ṭūr, 52:9

that '*mawr*' is a movement it would be a similar meaning but not exact, as the word means a quick, silent movement. Likewise, to say '*waḥy*' (revelation) means to inform, or that the verse ***'We have revealed to you'*** means 'We sent down', or that the verse:

وَقَضَيْنَآ إِلَىٰ بَنِىٓ إِسْرَٰٓءِيلَ

And We conveyed to the Children of Israel
Sūrah al-Isrā', 17:4

means 'We taught'. In all of these examples the substitute words are similar in meaning but not exact. Revelation is quick and secret and not just a way of informing. Conveying is much more specific than simply teaching as it involves information and revelation. It is common for the Arabs to attach a verb to another verb by using the preposition of the latter.

The author is stressing the point that all the words which have been mentioned as substitutes, '*mawr*' as movement, revelation as information, convey as taught etc. are all approximate in their meanings and not exact.

It is common for the Arabs to attach a verb to another verb by using the preposition of the latter. This is when one verb possesses the meaning of another and so the preposition of one can be used by the other. One of the clearest examples of this is the verse:

عَيْنًا يَشْرَبُ بِهَا عِبَادُ ٱللَّهِ

A spring of which the [righteous] servants of Allāh will drink
Sūrah al-Insān, 76:6

The word 'drink' also connotes the meaning of quenching thirst; it is not conceivable that they drink using the spring but rather using a cup. Therefore, some state the word '*bihā*' in the verse means 'from' [i.e. they drink from the spring]; while others state it means they quench their thirst from this spring. Hence, the verb here explicitly mentions drinking and also suggests another meaning which is the quenching of thirst, both using the preposition '*bihā*'.

From here, we can see the mistake made by those who substitute certain words with others, as they do in the verse:

قَالَ لَقَدْ ظَلَمَكَ بِسُؤَالِ نَعْجَتِكَ إِلَىٰ نِعَاجِهِۦ

[David] said, "He has certainly wronged you in demanding your ewe [in addition] to his ewes..."
Sūrah Ṣād, 38:24

substituting '*in addition to*' with '*with his ewes*'.

Likewise, in the verse:

مَنْ أَنصَارِىٓ إِلَى ٱللَّهِ

Who are my supporters for [the cause of] Allāh
Sūrah l-Imrān, 3:52

'*For the cause of*' has been substituted with '*with Allāh*' and so on.

The correct opinion is that of the grammarians of the Baṣrah School who state that it is a case of implication. Thus, the demand for the ewe implied taking and adding it to his ewes.

The scholars of Arabic grammar have differed in the case of a verb which is attached to a preposition which it would normally not be attached to. The correct opinion as mentioned is that the verb must then possess the meaning of another verb which would use such a preposition. Therefore, in the first verse, the demand for the ewe is not simply a demand, rather it is a demand to add this ewe to the others, so the preposition '*ilā*' (to) is correct and is not changed to '*maʿa*' (with). Likewise, in the second verse, the word '*ilā*' (to) is not changed to '*maʿa*' (with), [i.e. who are my supporters with Allāh], rather the meaning is 'who, along with me, will turn in repentance to Him.' For the supporters of Allāh are those who worship Him and repent to Him, as He states:

مُنِيبِينَ إِلَيۡهِ وَٱتَّقُوهُ

Turning in repentance to Him, and fear Him

Sūrah al-Rūm, 30:31

Another example is the verse:

وَإِن كَادُوا۟ لَيَفْتِنُونَكَ عَنِ ٱلَّذِىٓ أَوْحَيْنَآ إِلَيْكَ

And indeed, they were about to tempt you away from that which We revealed to you
Sūrah al-Isrā', 17:73

Tempt implies the meaning they prevent and divert you. Also [included in this is the following] verse:

وَنَصَرْنَٰهُ مِنَ ٱلْقَوْمِ ٱلَّذِينَ كَذَّبُوا۟ بِـَٔايَٰتِنَآ

And We aided [i.e. saved] him from the people who denied Our signs
Sūrah al-Anbiyā', 21:77

Aided also implies the meaning we saved and rescued. Likewise, another example is the verse:

عَيْنًا يَشْرَبُ بِهَا عِبَادُ ٱللَّهِ

...from which the servants of Allāh drink
Sūrah al-Insān, 76:6

Drinking implies the meaning of quenching one's thirst. Such examples are abundant.

Why is it that we make the verb imply an added meaning instead of changing the meaning of the preposition in order to fit that verb? The reason is that this allows us to give the verb an added meaning which makes it clearer.

As an example of this we can take the verse:

سَأَلَ سَآئِلٌۢ بِعَذَابٍ وَاقِعٍ ﴿١﴾

A supplicant asked concerning a punishment bound to happen
Sūrah al-Ma'ārij, 70:1

If we held the opinion that we change the preposition, the meaning would become: 'A supplicant asked about a punishment...' However, with the opinion we have chosen the meaning becomes: 'A supplicant asked concerning...' i.e. he was concerned and wished to know more about this impending punishment.

Likewise, whosoever says that '*rayb*' means '*shakk*' has only given an approximate meaning, for the word '*rayb*' implies internal unrest and turmoil as is in the *ḥadīth*: "*Leave that which is doubtful for that which is not doubtful.*"[31] As well as the *ḥadīth* in which the Prophet (ﷺ) passed by a deer with its head between its legs and said: "*None of you disturb [yuriyb] it.*"[32] Therefore, just as certainty implies inner peace and tranquillity its opposite, doubt, implies internal unrest and turmoil. On the other hand, the word '*shakk*' does not possess the same implications.

Also, in the statement of Allāh: ***"That Book"*** which is normally stated as meaning 'This Book' is another example of an approximate meaning. Even though what is being referred to in both statements is the Qur'ān, to point to something which is close by saying 'this' does not give the same implications and meanings as that which is referred to as being far and absent [which is implied by saying 'that']. Similarly, the word 'Book' is used here instead of 'Qur'ān' as it implies that it is comprehensively compiled, whereas the word 'Qur'ān' implies it is apparent and read. Such differences in language are present in the Qur'ān.

Here, the author – may Allāh have mercy upon him – mentions how sometimes the scholars explain a word by using another word which is approximate to it, not synonymous. This may be done in order to help clarify the intended meaning. The example given is ***"That Book"*** which can be explained as 'This Qur'ān'. Such an explanation is only meant to be approximate and not synonymous as the different words have different connotations.

[31] Collected by al-Bukhārī.

[32] *Sunan al-Nasā'ī*, no. 2817.

If one were to say that the word in the Qur'ān ***"an tubsala"*** means to be imprisoned, and another says it is to be bailed, this is not a contradictory difference, for the one imprisoned may or may not be bailed, so this is an approximate explanation.

To gather these varying sayings and opinions of the *salaf* is very beneficial. By gathering all these opinions one will have a clearer understanding of the intended meaning, much more so than if he were to just collect a saying or two.

This is because their varying statements concerning a single word enable a person to understand all the meanings that particular word implies. The most comprehensive book which gathers this is the *Tafsīr* of Ibn Jarīr [al-Ṭabarī] (may Allāh have mercy upon him), as he has managed to gather these sayings like none other. *Tafsīr Ibn Kathīr* is also similar in this regard as it is considered to be a summary of *Tafsīr al-Ṭabarī*. When they come to the explanation of a verse they mention who said what, the number of scholars who said that along with the chain of narration. The author mentions that such a collection of sayings is beneficial in ascertaining the meaning of the verse.

Even with all the above, there exist genuine differences of opinion amongst the *Salaf*, such as their differences in matters of jurisprudence. However, essential knowledge which everyone requires is known to all; the lay person and the elite. Examples of this include the number of daily prayers, the number of units (*rakʿahs*) in each prayer and their timings. Also known are the items on which *zakāt* is levied and their minimum amounts, which is the month of Ramaḍān, how to perform *ṭawāf*, the standing in ʿArafāt, stoning the pillars, where a person dons on the *iḥrām* etc.

Furthermore, the difference of opinion which existed amongst the companions in issues such as the shares of the grandfather and brothers[33] [in inheritance] and *musharrakah*,[34] rarely occur in the majority of inheritance rulings. Rather, most people only need to know about the shares of the ascendants, descendants, siblings and spouses. Indeed Allāh revealed three detailed verses concerning inheritance. In the first, He mentioned the ascendants and descendants. In the second, He mentioned the relatives who have prescribed shares such as the spouses and maternal brother. He mentioned in the third the relatives that have no prescribed shares and they are the full or paternal brothers. Cases in which the paternal grandfather and brothers meet are rare. This is why the first such reported instance in Islām took place after the death of the Prophet (ﷺ).

This difference of opinion may occur due to relevant evidences being hidden, overlooked, not being known or being misunderstood, or due to one favouring an opposing opinion. The purpose here is to briefly allude to this point and not to expound upon it.

---

[33] Translator's note: If the father of the deceased is also dead, and the deceased is survived by his paternal grandfather and full or paternal brothers, the scholars have differed concerning the shares which they receive. Some of the scholars state that the grandfather shares the estate with the brothers whilst others have said that the grandfather prevents the brothers from inheriting, just as the father would.

[34] Translator's note: This is when the deceased is survived by a husband, mother, two or more maternal brothers and any number of full brothers.

The author (may Allāh have mercy upon him) states here the reasons which may cause a difference of opinion; however these causes are not meant to be comprehensive, as this can be found in another of the author's works: *Rafʿ al-Malām ʿan al-A'imat al-Aʿlām* (Removing the Blame from the Great Scholars).

Here he states, 'due to relevant evidences being hidden', i.e. the scholar doesn't believe it is an evidence for that particular issue, so even though he came across the evidence, it didn't seem relevant to the issue at hand. Likewise, the evidence may be 'overlooked', meaning that even though he knew of the evidence he forgot it. If it is due to not being heard then that scholar was unaware of the evidence, or the difference may be due to misunderstanding the texts. The final cause mentioned here is due to the scholar knowing of the evidence, but due to another reason he avoids implementing it, such as the text being general and the scholar finding something which specifies it, or the text being limited in its application.

Whoever wishes to expound upon this topic should return to the author's work in this subject: *Rafʿ al-Malām ʿan al-A'imat al-Aʿlām* and also our book which is a summary of the authors with clearer examples: *Differences of opinion amongst the scholars – Their causes and our position towards them.*[35]

[35] Available in English, published by al-Hidaayah Publishing and Distribution.

Chapter 4

The Two Categories of Differences in the Exegesis of the Qur'ān Relating to the Source: Narrations and Deductions

Differences in the exegesis can be of two types: The source of the first is narrations and the other type is derived from different means, for knowledge is either a truthful narration, or a correct deduction, and the narrations either originate from one who is infallible or one who is not.

Here, we will discuss these narrations irrespective of whether they stem from an infallible authority or not; this is the first category. At times, we are able to distinguish between authentic and weak narrations and at times we are unable to do so. This latter part whose authenticity we cannot ascertain, for the most is unbeneficial and to delve into it is unnecessary.

As for that knowledge which is essential to the Muslims, then Allāh has placed for them sufficient signs showing them the truth. An example of that which is unbeneficial and has no clear evidence is the difference regarding the colour of the dog belonging to the companions of the cave. Similar to this is the difference regarding which part of the cow was used to strike the slain man.

Also included in this are the measurements of the ark of Nūḥ, and the type of wood used.

This is correct. Differing over the colour of the dog of the companions of the cave possesses no benefit, whether it was red, white or black it is unbeneficial to us and we have no way of correctly ascertaining this, unless we use Israelite traditions (*Isrā'īliyyīn*), and these traditions are not trustworthy. Therefore, there is no benefit in this and its colour makes no difference.

Similarly, another example is the part of the cow used by Mūsā to strike the slain man in the verse:

فَقُلْنَا اضْرِبُوهُ بِبَعْضِهَا ۚ

So We said, "Strike him [i.e. the slain man] with part of it."
Sūrah al-Baqarah, 2:73

Is the part being referred to the arm, leg, neck or head? There is no way to ascertain this.

[Concerning the ark of Nūḥ] there is no benefit in knowing where the wood came from or what type it was, did it come from the tamarisk or was it teal? What was its height, length and width? All of this is unbeneficial.

Similar to this is the name of the boy killed by Khiḍr etc. All this can only be ascertained from narrations. That which is authentically narrated from the Prophet (ﷺ) in this regard, such as the name of the companion of Mūsā being Khiḍr[36] is accepted. As for other than this, such as that which is taken from the People of the Book, like the narrations of Kaʿb, Wahb, Muḥammad ibn Isḥāq[37] and others who take from them, one cannot accept or reject these narrations except with clear proof.

It is reported in the *Ṣaḥīḥ* that the Prophet (ﷺ) said: "*If the People of the Book narrate to you then do not attest to their truthfulness nor reject them, rather say we believe in Allāh and His Messengers. Otherwise you may reject something truthful or attest to something false.*"[38]

Likewise, if narrations of the *tābiʿūn* - irrespective of whether or not they are taken from the People of the Book - differ then some of their sayings do not hold greater weight and authority than others. Rather, authentic narrations from the companions in this regard are more reliable than narrations from their students, as it is a stronger possibility that the companion heard his opinion from the Prophet (ﷺ) or from another of the companions who in turn heard it from the Prophet (ﷺ). Furthermore, the companions' narrations from the People of the Book are less than that of the *tābiʿūn*.

---

[36] See *Sahih al-Bukharī*, no. 74 and *Sahih Muslim*, no. 2380.

[37] Kaʿb al-Aḥbār, lived at the time of the companions. He narrated prophetic *ḥadīth* from the companions, and they narrated from him stories of the Prophets. He died in Hams in the year 32AH during the Caliphate of ʿUthmān.
Wahb ibn Munabbih was born towards the end of the Caliphate of ʿUthmān. He narrated from ʿAbdullāh ibn ʿAbbās and Ibn ʿUmar, and in turn was narrated by ʿAmr ibn Dīnār and his contemporaries. He became judge of Sanʿā and was known for quoting Israelite traditions. He authored a book on the topic of qadr and later retracted it. Other than this he was considered to be trustworthy in his narrations, and his narrations from his brother Hamām are collected in the two *Ṣaḥīḥs*. He died in the year 114AH.
Muḥammad ibn Isḥāq, a scholar specialising in history and battles. Ibn Maʿīn said: Trustworthy but not sufficient on his own. Aḥmad said: His *ḥadīth* are sound. He died in the year 151AH.

[38] See *Sahīh al-Bukhārī*, no. 4485.

Therefore, when a companion adamantly holds an opinion, it is not thought that he has taken this opinion from the People of the Book, especially since they were forbidden from believing them. The point being, such differences [in opinion] in which one cannot ascertain what is authentic and what is weak is just as unbeneficial as narrating a *ḥadīth* in which one cannot ascertain its authenticity.

As for the first category in which one is able to establish the authenticity of a narration, this is possible – and all praise is for Allāh – in those matters which are essential. Many narrations in *tafsīr*, *ḥadīth* and expeditions concerning the Prophet (ﷺ) and other Prophets are false as they contradict authentic narrations. This is the case with narrations and what is deduced by other methods.

The point being, there are clear signs showing the authenticity or weakness of those narrations which are essential and required by the Muslims. It is also known that many narrations in *tafsīr* are similar to narrations about expeditions and history. This is why Imām Aḥmad said: "Three things contain no chain of narration (*isnād*): *tafsīr*, expeditions and history." This is because the majority of narrations are *marāsīl*,[39] such as that which is mentioned by ʿUrwah ibn Zubayr,[40] al-Shaʿbī,[41] al-Zuhrī,[42]

[39] Translator's note: The definition of *mursal* will be given by Shaykh Ibn ʿUthaymīn shortly.

[40] ʿUrwah was one of the seven jurists of Madīnah. He was born in the year 29 AH and died in the year 93 AH. He took his knowledge from his aunt ʿĀ'ishah, ʿAlī, Muḥammad ibn Aslam and Abū Hurayrah. He was one who stayed away from trials, a trustworthy scholar.

[41] He is ʿĀmir ibn Sharāḥbīl al-Shaʿbī, died in the year 103 AH. This great *imām* met five hundred companions and was a judge for ʿUmar ibn ʿAbdul-ʿAzīz. He is from the teachers of Ibn Sīrīn, Aʿmash and Shuʿbah. Al-Fajalī said: His *mursal ḥadīth* are authentic.

[42] He is Muḥammad ibn Muslim ibn Shihāb al-Zuhrī; born in the year 50 AH and died in the year 124 AH. He was one of the great scholars of the Ḥijāz and Shām. He was the first to pen in the field of *ḥadīth* at the request of ʿUmar ibn ʿAbdul-ʿAzīz, and would say about himself: 'I have never forgotten anything I've memorised'. He was from the teachers of Imām Mālik, Layth and their contemporaries.

Mūsā ibn ʿUqbah,[43] Ibn Isḥāq, and those who came after them such as Yaḥyā ibn Saʿīd,[44] Walīd ibn Muslim,[45] al-Wāqidī[46] and others who authored in history and expeditions. Indeed, the most knowledgeable of people concerning military expeditions are the people of Madīnah, then Shām and then Iraq.

This is an important point of benefit. People from a certain place or a certain group may be more knowledgeable than others in a particular field or subject. Therefore, if you are asked: Who is the most knowledgeable about military expeditions? The answer is as the author stated: The people of Madīnah, followed by the people of Shām and then the people of Iraq. The author further comments upon this by saying:

[43] Mūsā ibn ʿUqbah was one of the oldest historians of Madīnah. He learnt from ʿUrwah ibn Zubayr and ʿAlqamah ibn Waqqāṣ. Mālik said about him: 'Take the narrations of Ibn ʿUqbah concerning the expeditions, for he was trustworthy and his narrations are the most authentic'. He died during the Caliphate of ʿAbdul-Malik.

[44] Yaḥyā ibn Saʿīd ibn Abān ibn Saʿīd, the *ḥāfiẓ*. He learnt from his father, Hishām ibn ʿUrwah and Ibn Jurayḥ. His students include his son, Saʿīd ibn Yaḥyā, Imām Aḥmad, Isḥāq and Ibn Maʿīn. He died in the year 194 AH.

[45] Al-Walīd ibn Muslim, Abul-ʿAbbās, the scholar of Damascus. From amongst his teachers are Muhammad ibn ʿAjlān, Hishām ibn Ḥassān and al-Awzāʿī. His students include Imām Aḥmad, Isḥāq and Ibn Madyan. He died in the year 195 AH.

[46] Abū ʿAbdullāh Muḥammad ibn ʿUmar ibn Wāqid al-Wāqidī, he was one of the great scholars, the judge of Iraq. He studied under Ibn ʿAjlān, Ibn Jurayḥ and Mālik and he taught the likes of Ibn Saʿd and Aḥmad ibn Manṣūr. He was a scholar in expeditions, biographies and conquests. Ibrāhīm al-Ḥarbī said: 'He is the trustworthy representative for Islām; however the scholars of *ḥadīth* do not rate him as highly in narrations'. He died in the year 207 AH.

The people of Madīnah are the most knowledgeable in this as the expeditions took place among them. The people of Shām are known for their military and tactical skills, and due to this they possess an understanding of these matters which others don't. For this reason, people revere Abū Isḥāq's book on this topic, and consider al-Awzāʿī[47] to be more knowledgeable in this field than other scholars.

The author here has made special mention of Abū Isḥāq al-Fizārī and al-Awzāʿī.

[47] ʿAbdul-Raḥmān ibn ʿAmr al-Awzāʿī, he was one of the great scholars of the Muslims, a role-model in his knowledge and understanding in Shām. He studied under the likes of ʿAṭā', Ibn Sīrīn and Qatādah, and taught many of the scholars of *ḥadīth* and jurisprudence of his time. Isḥāq ibn Rāḥawayh said: 'If Awzāʿī, Thawrī and Mālik agree on something then it is the *Sunnah*'. He died in the year 175 AH.

As for *tafsīr*, then the most knowledgeable of people in this field are the people of Makkah. The reason for this is that they are the students of Ibn 'Abbās, like Mujāhid,[48] 'Aṭā' ibn Abū Rabāḥ[49] and 'Ikrimah,[50] and others such as Ṭāwūs,[51] Abū Sha'thā'[52] and Sa'īd ibn Jubayr. Likewise it includes the people of Kūfah who are from the students of 'Abdullāh ibn Mas'ūd.

The author (may the mercy of Allāh be upon him) states: The most knowledgeable of people regarding *tafsīr* are the people of Makkah, just as the people of Madīnah are knowledgeable in military expeditions. The reason for this is that people like Mujāhid and 'Aṭā' were students of Ibn 'Abbās (☬).

---

[48] Mujāhid ibn Jabr al-Makkī, the freed slave of al-Sā'ib ibn al-Sā'ib. He was born in the year 21 AH, and died while in prostration in the year 102 AH. He studied under Ibn 'Abbās, Umm Salamah, Abū Hurayrah and Jābir, and was teacher of the likes of 'Ikrimah, 'Aṭā' and Qatādah. Ibn Ma'īn and Abū Zur'ah both classed him as trustworthy. It is narrated that he went through the Qur'ān with Ibn 'Abbās three times.

[49] 'Aṭā' ibn Abū Rabāḥ was originally from Yemen. He moved to Makkah and excelled in jurisprudence, and was the leading authority of his time in Makkah. Ibn 'Abbās would say: 'You come to me even though among you is 'Aṭā''. He died in 114 AH.

[50] 'Ikrimah the freed slave of Ibn 'Abbās. Al-Sha'bī said: 'There is no one left more knowledgeable about the Book of Allāh than 'Ikrimah'. He passed away in the year 105 AH.

[51] Ṭāwūs ibn Kaysān was also originally from Yemen. He met fifty of the companions, and became one of the great scholars. He also studied with some of the great students of the companions. Ibn 'Abbās said: 'Indeed, I think Ṭāwūs is from the people of Paradise'. He died in the year 106 AH.

[52] His full name is Jābir ibn Zayd al-Azdī al-Baṣrī. Ibn 'Abbās said about him: 'He is from the scholars'. He died in the year 93 AH.

Some of these [mentioned above] are distinguished scholars. From the scholars of Madīnah who specialised in *tafsīr* is Zayd ibn Aslam.[53] His students include Imām Mālik, and his own son ʿAbdul-Raḥmān. ʿAbdul-Raḥmān was the teacher of ʿAbdullāh ibn Wahb.

Mursal ḥadīth which are reported by many narrators to the extent that there can be no chance of intentional or incidental collusion between the narrators, are without doubt authentic. A narration can be authentic and correct, or false in which the narrator intentionally lied or made a mistake. If we can establish that it is free of lies and mistakes then it is undoubtedly authentic.

Are *mursal ḥadīth* authentic and correct or not? A *mursal ḥadīth* is when the one narrating from the Prophet (ﷺ) did not hear from him, whether it is a companion or a *tābiʿī*. For example, if Muḥammad ibn Abū Bakr narrated a *ḥadīth* from the Prophet (ﷺ) we would class it as *mursal*. He never heard from him as he was born in the year of the Farewell Pilgrimage. Despite this being the case the scholars state the *mursal ḥadīth* of companions is sufficient as evidence. As for the *tābiʿūn*, it differs from person to person; some are accepted while others are not. As for those who are known to only narrate from companions such as Saʿīd ibn al-Mussayib, who it is said only narrates *mursal ḥadīth* from Abū Hurayrah, then his *mursal* is authentic. However, those not of this stature must have each of their narrations taken on its individual merit. If the narration has a number of narrators and it has been accepted then it is also classed as authentic. An example of this is the *ḥadīth* of ʿAmr ibn Ḥazm that the Prophet (ﷺ) wrote a letter to the people of Yemen instructing them in matters of blood money and *Zakāt*, and in it he wrote: *"Let none except those in a state of purity touch the Qur'ān."*[54]

---

[53] Zayd ibn Aslam died in 136 AH. He was a very distinguished scholar of the Qur'ān from among the students of Ubayy ibn Kʿab.

[54] See *Muwaṭṭa' Mālik*, vol. 1, p. 199.

Therefore, if a *ḥadīth* has been narrated from two or more chains and it is known that the narrators did not conspire in its differences, and that it is not possible to agree on such a thing incidentally, the narration is classed as authentic. It is like a person who mentions an incident which took place, explaining in detail what was said and done, and then another person who cannot have conspired with the first mentions the exact same story in detail. It is known that on the whole the story is true. If they had conspired to lie about the story or had mistakenly done so, it would not be conceivable that they would agree on all the details, as without collusion such a thing would be impossible.

It is possible that a person may compose a verse of poetry and another happens to also compose the same verse, or one tells a particular lie which happens to be the same lie another tells without having colluded with the first. However, if a person was to compose a lengthy poem containing all types of rhythmical styles and techniques, it is not possible that someone else would compose the exact same poem with the same words and meanings, rather it is known that the latter took from the former. Likewise, if someone mentions a long narration containing much detail and another person narrates the same thing, then the latter either colluded with the former, or he copied him, or else the narration is true. Using this method it is possible to determine the authenticity of narrations which are reported through different transmissions, even though each individual narration is not sufficient on its own due to a missing link present or the weakness of a narrator.

The author (may Allāh have mercy upon him) states that if a *mursal ḥadīth* has been reported with a number of different chains of narration, and there is no collusion or accidental agreement possible then the narration is classified as authentic. He then gave an example of this: A person narrates an incident to you mentioning details such as what was said and done, and who was present, however you do not deem such a person trustworthy. Then a second person came and narrated the same incident with the same details, and you know that he cannot have colluded with the first, and then a third and fourth also come with the same story. Even if each individual was not trustworthy on his own, the fact that they have all agreed on such a lengthy story signifies that it is true.

If on the other hand, it was a short story which was narrated by a number of people, and the narrators are not trustworthy then it is possible that they may have collaborated with one another. For example, if they wish to deceive people, one may claim that a missile landed in a certain place without giving any precise details, and another may also come with the same general story. It is possible here that such a story was planned in order to deceive. However, a lengthy and detailed description would be more convincing, unless we know that the narrators colluded with another.

This is briefly what the author has mentioned here. He is stressing how a *mursal ḥadīth* due to its different chains may become authentic. In terms of a *mursal ḥadīth*, all the narrators are attributing the *ḥadīth* to the Prophet (ﷺ), and the fact they all agree on this makes it more likely that it is indeed a prophetic *ḥadīth*, as it is not plausible that the likes of these narrators would all attribute something to the Prophet (ﷺ) without any basis.

Also note that the author emphasises the above as being something which people can relate to, and does not use intellect as the basis of his reasoning but rather the norm and custom of people. This is because matters such as narrations are not judged by intellect, as Ibn Ḥajar mentions.

However this method cannot be used in pinpointing the accuracy of words and details; the accuracy of such things must be established via another method.

The above mentioned method alluded to by the author is not sufficient in guaranteeing the accuracy of words and details, rather a more authentic method must be employed for such things.

Here, the author is not discussing *mursal ḥadīth*, but incidents and narrations in general. Accuracy in words and details must be established using an authentic method. Therefore, the general outline of the incident can be validated via this method, but the accuracy of the details requires a more stringent method.

Thus, the battle of Badr has been established by recurring narrations. It is established that it took place before the battle of Uḥud. Furthermore, it is also established that Ḥamzah, ʿAlī and Abū ʿUbaydah had a duel with ʿUtbah, Shaybah and Walīd, that ʿAlī killed Walīd, and Ḥamzah killed his opponent. However there is a difference [of opinion] over who his opponent was, was it ʿUtbah or Shaybah?

This is an essential principal to remember, and is very beneficial in determining the truthfulness of narrations in *ḥadīth*, *tafsīr* and military expeditions, and what people said or did. For this reason, if a prophetic *ḥadīth* has been narrated with two different chains, and it is known that one narrator did not collaborate with the other, we can be certain that the narration is true. This is even more so if the narrators are those who would not intentionally lie, rather the most that is feared for them is that they may make a mistake or forget.

The one who is familiar with companions such as Ibn Masʿūd, Ubayy ibn Kaʿb,[55] Ibn ʿUmar, Jābir,[56] Abū Saʿīd[57] and Abū Hurayrah[58] would know that they would never intentionally ascribe a lie to the Prophet (ﷺ), let alone those who are greater in status than them. This is similar to a person who knows another well due to his extensive experiences with him. He knows he would not steal, ambush or give false testimonies.

This can also be said about the *tābiʿūn* of Madīnah, Makkah, Shām and Baṣrah. Whoever is familiar with the likes of Abū

---

[55] Ubayy ibn Kʿab al-Anṣārī, one of the scribes of the Qur'ān who later taught it in Madinah. He died during the reign of ʿUmar.

[56] Jābir ibn ʿAbdullāh, died 78 AH. He was one of the most prolific transmitters of *ḥadīth*.

[57] Abū Saʿīd Saʿd ibn Mālik al-Khudrī, one of the companions who was constantly in the service of the Prophet at different times and a prolific narrator of *ḥadīth*.

[58] Abū Hurayrah, died 58 AH. He was the greatest narrator of *ḥadīth*; his narrations number well over a thousand.

Ṣāliḥ al-Sammān,[59] al-Aʿraj,[60] Sulaymān ibn Yasār,[61] Zayd ibn Aslam and their contemporaries will know that they would not purposefully ascribe lies to the Prophet (ﷺ), let alone those scholars who are greater than them such as Muḥammad ibn Sīrīn,[62] al-Qāsim ibn Muḥammad,[63] Saʿīd ibn al-Musayyib,[64] ʿAlqamah,[65] al-Aswad[66] and others.

Rather what is feared is that they may have made errors, as mistakes and forgetfulness often affect people. However, certain scholars are known to be far from this. This is known about the likes of al-Shaʿbī, al-Zuhrī, ʿUrwah, Qatādah[67] and al-Thawrī,[68] especially al-Zuhrī and al-Thawrī in their times. It is said: 'Indeed,

---

[59] His name is Dhakwān. He narrated from some of the companions. Aʿmash narrated a thousand *ḥadīth* from him. Imām Aḥmad said concerning him: 'very trustworthy'. He died in the year 101 AH.

[60] ʿAbdul-Raḥmān ibn Hurmuz, the reciter. He studied under some of the companions. His students include al-Zuhrī, Muḥammad ibn Muslim and Abū Zinād. Imām al-Bukhārī stated: 'The most authentic of chains are Abū Zinād from al-Aʿraj from Abū Hurayrah'. He died in Alexandria in the year 117 AH.

[61] He was one of the seven jurists of Madīnah. He was the teacher of Qatādah, al-Zuhrī and ʿAmr ibn Shuʿayb. He died around the year 100 AH at the age of 73.

[62] Muḥammad ibn Sīrīn was the freed slave of Anas. He studied under some of the companions and taught a number of leading *tābiʿūn*. Ibn Saʿd said: 'He was trustworthy, a distinguished and great scholar and jurist, possessing vast knowledge'. He died in the year 110AH.

[63] The grandson of Abū Bakr and one of the seven jurists of Madīnah. Abū Zinād said: 'I have never seen anyone more knowledgeable of the *Sunnah* than him'. He died in the year 106 AH.

[64] Saʿīd ibn al-Musayyib, one of the leading, most distinguished and most knowledgeable scholars of the *tābiʿūn*. ʿAbdullāh ibn ʿUmar said: 'He is, by Allāh, one who is followed.' Abū Ḥātim said: 'The most trustworthy narrator from Abū Hurayrah.' He died in the year 93 AH.

[65] ʿAlqamah ibn Qays al-Nakhaʿī; he narrated from the four rightly guided caliphs and their generation. He died in the year 62 AH.

[66] Al-Aswad ibn Yazīd ibn Qays, he was a student of Ibn Masʿūd, ʿĀ'ishah and Abū Mūsā. It is said he would finish the Qur'ān every two nights, and that he performed Hajj eighty times. He died in the year 74 AH.

[67] Qatādah ibn Diʿāmah al-Baṣrī. He narrated from Anas, Saʿīd ibn al-Musayyib and Ibn Sīrīn. He died in the year 117 AH.

[68] Sufyān al-Thawrī al-Kūfī. He was one of the great scholars known for his memorisation, knowledge and piety. He passed away in the year 161 AH.

Ibn Shihāb al-Zuhrī rarely erred even though he narrated many *ḥadīths*.'

The point here is that if a *ḥadīth* has been narrated from two different chains without collaboration, then it cannot be a mistake or a lie. A lengthy story cannot be one big mistake; rather parts of it may contain errors. Therefore, if a person narrates a long and detailed story, and another narrates exactly the same story without collusion then both stories cannot be a mistake, just as they cannot be lies. As such, the mistakes which occur can be concerning certain details within the story, like the *ḥadīth* in which the Prophet (ﷺ) bought a camel from Jābir. Whoever contemplates the different chains of the *ḥadīth* will realise that the *ḥadīth* is authentic, even though the narrations differ concerning the exact price of the camel.

We have already mentioned this point. The accuracy of details within a story must be established via a more authentic and trustworthy method.

This is also explained by al-Bukhārī in his *Ṣaḥīḥ*, for the majority of what is in *Bukhārī* and *Muslim* can be ascribed to the Prophet (ﷺ) with certainty, as it is of this calibre, and the *Ummah* has accepted it as such, and the whole Muslim nation cannot unite upon error. For if a *ḥadīth* is a lie but the *Ummah* accepts it as truthful, they have in essence accepted a lie. This is unity upon error and is impossible. Without unity and consensus it is possible that a narration contains a mistake or lie, just as this is possible in an analogy in which the truth may be in the opposite of what we believed. However, once unity is achieved upon a matter, we affirm its wording and meaning.

This is clear, for sometimes you may come across a *ḥadīth* and know that the meaning is such and such, but there is a slight possibility that there is another implicit meaning which is being referred to. However, once consensus is reached that the intended meaning is the apparent one; the implicit meaning can be disregarded as the *Ummah* does not unite upon error.

For example, the difference in narrations over the exact price of Jābir's camel does not cause the *ḥadīth* to become disordered (*muḍṭarib*),[69] as this disorder is not in the basis of the *ḥadīth* but in some of the details which ultimately do not have an effect on the overall *ḥadīth*. Similar to this is the difference present in the *ḥadīth* of Fuḍālah ibn ʿUbayd concerning the price of the necklace; was it twelve *dīnārs*, or more or less? This difference also has no bearing as it does not affect the basis of the story.

[69] Translator's note: This is a *ḥadīth* on which a number of reports with the same strength differ; thus, neither compromise nor abrogation can be applied.

For this reason, the majority of scholars from all of the different schools of thought agree that if a *ḥadīth* reported with a single narrator in its chain of narration is accepted or approved by action then it is sufficient as evidence. This is mentioned by the authors of *Uṣūl al-Fiqh* (principles of jurisprudence) from all the schools of *fiqh*: the students of Abū Ḥanīfah, Mālik, Shāfiʿī and Aḥmad. This opinion is opposed by a minority of latter time scholars who chose the opinion of some theologians. However, the majority of theologians agree with the jurists, scholars of *ḥadīth* and predecessors on this.

This is the opinion of the majority of Ashʿarite scholars such as Abū Isḥāq and Ibn Fawrak.[70] Ibn al-Bāqillānī is the one who held the opposing opinion, and was followed by Abul-Maʿālī,[71] Abū Ḥāmid,[72] Ibn ʿAqīl,[73] Ibn al-Jawzī,[74] Ibn al-Khaṭīb,[75] al- Āmadī[76] and others. The first opinion is also supported by Abū Ḥāmid, Abu al-Ṭayyib, Abu Isḥāq and their likes from the Shāfiʿī school, Qaḍī ʿAbdul-Wahhāb and his likes from the Mālikī school, Shams ul-Dīn al-Sarakhsī and others from the Ḥanafī school, and Abū Yaʿlā, Abul-Khaṭṭāb, and Abul-Ḥasan from the Ḥanbalī school.

Here, the author has made mention of the scholars of all four *madhabs*, and this shows his vast knowledge in various fields. This

[70] Muḥammad ibn al-Ḥasan al-Iṣfahānī, died 406 AH. He was an Ashʿarī scholar in theology who followed the Shāfiʿī school of law.

[71] Abul-Maʿālī ʿAbdul-Malik al-Juwaynī famously known as *Imām al-Ḥaramayn*. He died in 478 AH and was the teacher of Imām al-Ghazālī.

[72] Abū Ḥamid al-Ghazālī, the famous scholar noted for his many works in various disciplines, especially known for his criticism of Greek philosophy and the defense of the Islamic faith.

[73] ʿAlī ibn ʿAqīl, died 513 AH. He was a great Ḥanbalī scholar from Baghdad.

[74] Abul-Farj, ʿAbdul-Raḥmān ibn al-Jawzī who died in 597 AH. He was a great Ḥanbalī scholar and a prolific writer. His works exceed three hundred volumes.

[75] Aḥmad ibn ʿAlī, commonly known as al-Khaṭīb al-Baghdādī, died in 463 AH. He was most famous for his history of Baghdad in fourteen volumes.

[76] Abul-Ḥasan ʿAlī ibn Muḥammad al-Āmadī. He was born and raised in Baghdad, taught in Egypt and later died in Damascus in 631 AH.

issue is an issue which pertains to the principles of jurisprudence and the science of *ḥadīth*. If a narration with a single narrator is accepted or acted upon, does that then signify certainty and knowledge regarding that narration? There is a difference of opinion regarding this as the author mentions; the majority hold the opinion that it is sufficient. Ibn Ḥajar states that it is only sufficient as evidence when there are signs which attest to this, and this is the correct opinion.

No one doubts that the Prophet (ﷺ) said: "*Verily, actions are only judged by their intentions, and for everyone is that which they intended,*"[77] even though its chain possesses a single narrator. Likewise, we don't doubt that the Prophet (ﷺ) said: "*Whoever performs an action [whose basis] is not from us will have it rejected,*"[78] even though it has only a single narrator in its chain. Even though these and similar *ḥadīths* only have single narrators in their chains, they are sufficient as evidence due to their many supporting evidences and due to the *Ummah* accepting them.

[77] *Sahih al-Bukharī*, no. 1 and *Sahih Muslim*, no. 1907.

[78] *Sahih Muslim*, no. 1718.

If consensus upon a narration is sufficient in establishing it, then the consensus which is applicable is that of the scholars of *ḥadīth*. Just as consensus in practical rulings is sought with the scholars who specialise in orders, prohibitions and recommendations, so is the case with this.

The author here is stressing that the consensus sought in each field is with the specialists of that field. In the science of *ḥadīth* we seek the consensus of the scholars of *ḥadīth*, so if those scholars agree that a narration with a single narrator in its chain is sufficient as evidence when accepted by the *Ummah* and supported by other signs, then we pay no attention to others [outside this speciality] who may oppose this opinion. Likewise, the consensus sought in rulings – what is obligatory, prohibited, recommended, disliked etc. – is with the scholars who specialise in this, i.e. the jurists. Similarly, in grammatical issues consensus is sought with the grammarians, and so on.

The reason for this is that a specialist in a field is more knowledgeable in that field than others. Therefore, a jurist does not know about the consensus of grammarians, or the scholars of *ḥadīth* etc. Therefore, we apply the consensus of the scholars of each field in their field. If the jurists claim that a narration with a single narrator in its chain is not sufficient as evidence, we ignore this opposition; rather we seek the consensus of the scholars of *ḥadīth* in this issue.

The point being made is that a narration possessing multiple transmissions in which no collusion or agreement is possible, is sufficient in establishing the content narrated. This is more beneficial when one is aware of the state of the narrators.

If, for example, a grammarian was to state: 'The scholars have agreed upon the obligation of covering the *'awrah* in the prayer,' we would reply that this is not your speciality. Rather mention the different grammatical positions of verbs etc. and we will agree with this. This is why the author mentions: This is more beneficial when one is aware of the state of the narrators, meaning is the one who is narrating from the jurists, grammarians or scholars of principles of jurisprudence?

In this regard, one may benefit from the narrations of an unknown narrator or one possessing bad memory, or a *mursal ḥadīth*. For this reason the scholars would write down such narrations and say: 'What can't be used as evidence itself may be used in order to support another evidence'. Imām Aḥmad would state: 'I may write the narrations of a man in order to consider them.' He then gave ʿAbdullāh ibn Lahiyʿah, the Egyptian judge as an example of such a man. He was a pious man who narrated many *ḥadīths*, but when his books were burnt, his later narrations had mistakes in them, so he was a narrator who was considered and used to support others. He is often compared to al-Layth ibn Saʿd;[79] Layth was a trustworthy authority and *imām*.

Here, the statement of Imām Aḥmad is mentioned, 'I may write the narrations of a man in order to consider them.' To consider them here does not mean to use them as evidence, but to use them as supporting evidences. Ibn Ḥajar said: 'To consider is to follow the different narrations.' Here we have two terms, a *shāhid* and a *mutābiʿ*. A *shāhid* is when we use a different *ḥadīth* with a different chain of narration as supporting evidence for the *ḥadīth* we wish to support. A *mutābiʿ* takes place in the same chain of narration, meaning that a narrator is supported by another narrator in his narration. For example, if an untrustworthy narrator narrated from al-Zuhrī, and al-Zuhrī is trustworthy, we must look for another person who will support the untrustworthy narrator in his narration from al-Zuhrī. If we find a strong narrator then he is used to support the first. The example of a *shāhid* would be when we find a different narration other than al-Zuhrī's which states the same as his narration. This is what is being referred to in Imām Aḥmad's statement: '...in order to consider them,' i.e. in order to consider whether there is a *shāhid* or *mutābiʿ* which supports this narration.

[79] Abul-Ḥārith al-Layth ibn Sʿad, died 175 AH. He was the most famous scholar of Egypt in his time. He was also a *faqīh* of some eminence being classed as more proficient than Imām Mālik by al-Shāfiʿī.

This is the reason why Imām Aḥmad often uses the narration of ʿAbdullāh ibn Lahiyʿah in his *Musnad*. Whoever heard from him before his books were burnt is considered to be strong in terms of evidence. Whoever heard from him after his books were burnt, his narrations are doubtful and not trustworthy, as the state of this *imām* changed after this incident. If we are unable to determine whether the one narrating from Ibn Lahiyʿah heard from him before or after his books were burnt, we cease to pass judgement. However, the narrations of the second category are considered to be wrong.

Just as they use the *ḥadīths* of the one with bad memory as supporting evidence, they may also classify the *ḥadīth* of a trustworthy and reliable narrator as weak due to apparent and clear errors found in some narrations. This is known as the science of *ʿilal al-ḥadīth* (the hidden defects in *ḥadīth*), and is one of the most noble and advanced sciences in the field of *ḥadīth*. This is when one who is usually trustworthy and reliable makes an error in his narrations, and his error has become known.

It is known that the Prophet (ﷺ) married Maymūnah whilst he was not in a state of *iḥrām*,[80] and that he prayed two *rakʿahs* inside the *Kaʿbah*.[81] The narrations of Ibn ʿAbbās which state that he (ﷺ) married whilst in a state of *iḥrām*[82] and that he did not pray inside the *Kaʿbah* are mistaken. Likewise, it is also known that the Prophet (ﷺ) only performed four *ʿUmrahs*,[83] and that the statement of Ibn ʿUmar which claims he made *ʿUmrah* in Rajab is also mistaken.

Even though these are all trustworthy narrators, no one is safe from making mistakes. Therefore, the Prophet (ﷺ) married Maymūnah whilst not in the state of *iḥrām*, as this was attested to by Maymūnah herself, and by Abū Rāfiʿ who was the emissary between the two. Likewise, the narration which mentions that he prayed inside the *Kaʿbah* is also established. The opposing narration of Ibn ʿAbbās at the most, implies he had no knowledge of this event.

Similarly, it is also established that the Prophet (ﷺ) performed four *ʿUmrahs*. The *ʿUmrah* of Ḥudaybiyyah, the *ʿUmrah* of Qaḍā', the *ʿUmrah* from Jiʿirrānah and the *ʿUmrah* performed with his farewell *Ḥajj*. These are the only four *ʿUmrahs* he performed. The statement of Ibn ʿUmar that he also performed *ʿUmrah* in Rajab is a mistake which he made.

---

[80] *Sunan al-Tirmidhī*, no. 841.

[81] Collected by Aḥmad in *al-Musnad*.

[82] *Sahih al-Bukhāri*, no. 4258 and *Sahih Muslim*, no. 1410.

[83] *Sahih al-Bukhāri*, no. 1775 and 1776.

It is also well known that the Prophet (ﷺ) performed *tamattuʿ* in a state of security during his farewell *Ḥajj*. Thus, the narration in which ʿUthmān said to ʿAlī: 'We were in a state of fear on that day'[84] is also mistaken.

ʿUthmān (ؓ) did not see the validity of *tamattuʿ*. Thus he stated that the only reason the Prophet (ﷺ) performed it was due to being in a state of fear. However this is incorrect, as the Prophet (ﷺ) performed *tamattuʿ* whilst being as safe as one can be.

[84] *Sahih Muslim*, no. 1223.

Another example of this is what is reported in some narrations in *Ṣaḥīḥ al-Bukhārī*: *"The Hellfire will not be full until Allāh creates another creation for it."* This is also a narration which contains a mistake.

This example is also known to contain a mistake, and that is that after the inhabitants of the Fire have entered into it, there will still remain some space in it, so Allāh will create another creation in order to fill it. This is incorrect. The Fire will continue to be filled and will continue to say: 'Is there more?' until Allāh places His foot over it. Then it will constrict and say 'Enough, enough.' Furthermore, if Allāh was to create another creation just to fill the Fire with them this would contradict His justice and mercy. Therefore, it is realised that this narration is incorrect even if it is present in *Ṣaḥīḥ al-Bukhārī*, and the narrator has made a mistake.

People are of two extremes in this issue. A group of scholastic theologians and their likes who are unfamiliar with the science of *ḥadīth* and its scholars, do not differentiate between authentic and weak narrations. This causes them to doubt the authenticity of *ḥadīths* even though they are classified as authentic by the scholars of this science. The other group claims to follow *ḥadīths* wherever they find a wording narrated by a trustworthy person, or a *ḥadīth* which appears to be authentic, considering it to be from among those *ḥadīths* whose authenticity has been established by the scholars. Even if they contradict a well known and authentic *ḥadīth*, they will instead revert to facile interpretations or insist it is an evidence for a certain issue even though the scholars of *ḥadīth* consider it to be incorrect.

This last statement by the author is something which many people fall into today. You find people depending upon the apparent chain of narration, correcting *ḥadīths* without focusing on those *ḥadīths* which are considered to be like the mountains of the *Sunnah*. This is an issue I am constantly warning about: If *ḥadīths* which are not found in the well known books of *ḥadīth* – even if they have an apparent authentic chain of narration – contradict *ḥadīths* which are found in such books and have been widely accepted, then the former should not be depended upon. Therefore, we do not only rely upon the chain of narration in determining the authenticity of a *ḥadīth*. Rather all these issues must be judged using the general principles of the *sharīʿah*. Here, the author clarifies that the chain of narration of a *ḥadīth* may be authentic but the text of the *ḥadīth* inauthentic. Likewise, certain people who claim to have knowledge in the field of *ḥadīth*, and claim to be scholars of this science, depend upon such *ḥadīths* which even though apparently authentic contradict those *ḥadīths* which are far more established and more widely accepted.

Just as there are signs by which one can come to know and establish that a *ḥadīth* is truthful, there are signs which also point to a *ḥadīth* being a fabrication. An example of this is what is narrated by the fabricators and people of innovation in certain matters of superiority (*faḍā'il*), such as the *ḥadīth* concerning the day of *ʿĀshūrā'* which states that whoever prays two *rakʿahs* will receive the reward of such and such prophets.

In the books of *tafsīr* many such fabrications exist. An example of this is the *ḥadīth* narrated by al-Thaʿlabī, al-Wāḥidī and al-Zamakhsharī regarding the superiority of the chapters of the Qur'ān. These are fabricated by the agreement of the scholars. Al-Thaʿlabī himself was a good and pious man, but he was like a wood gatherer at night. He would copy whatever he found in the books of *tafsīr*, whether authentic, weak or fabricated.

A wood gatherer at night does not distinguish between dry and moist wood, or even what may be wood or a snake; he just gathers what he finds.

Al-Wāḥidī was his companion and was more knowledgeable than him in the Arabic language, but more distant in terms of following the pious predecessors. Al-Baghawī's *tafsīr* is a summary of al-Tha'labī's. However, he preserved his book from fabricated *ḥadīths* and innovated opinions often found in other books of *tafsīr*.

This is a review of these books by Shaykh ul-Islām (may Allāh have mercy upon him); he mentioned the books of al-Tha'labī, al-Wāḥidī and al-Baghawī. The summary being that al-Baghawi's *tafsīr* is the best of the three.

If one were to ask: 'Does mentioning the chain of a narration of a fabricated *ḥadīth* vindicate placing it in a book of *tafsīr*?' I would reply that even though this frees him from blame, it should still be avoided. This is with regards to fabricated *ḥadīths*; weak *ḥadīths* are a lighter matter. However fabricated *ḥadīths* should be avoided.

Examples include the many *ḥadīths* mentioning that the *basmalah* is said aloud, and the long *ḥadīth* of ʿAlī where he gave his ring in charity whilst praying. These are considered fabricated by the agreement of the scholars.[85]

The *shaykh* is referring to the lengthy *ḥadīth* of ʿAlī, which is narrated via several transmissions and collected by al-Ṭabarī and others in the exegesis of the verse:

إِنَّمَا وَلِيُّكُمُ ٱللَّهُ وَرَسُولُهُۥ وَٱلَّذِينَ ءَامَنُواْ ٱلَّذِينَ يُقِيمُونَ ٱلصَّلَوٰةَ وَيُؤْتُونَ
ٱلزَّكَوٰةَ وَهُمْ رَٰكِعُونَ ﴿٥٥﴾

Your ally is none but Allāh and His Messenger and those who have believed – those who establish prayer and give zakāh, and they bow [in worship].
Sūrah al-Māʾidah, 5:55

The narration is that a poor man passed by ʿAlī (رضي الله عنه) whilst he was bowing (in *rukūʿ*), so he gave him his ring and this verse was revealed. Ibn Kathīr said concerning these narrations: ‘Absolutely none of these narrations are authentic due to their weak chains and unknown narrators.’ Aḥmad Shākir said regarding the narration found in al-Ṭabarī: ‘None of these narrations are sufficient as evidence.’ The author considers them to be fabricated, i.e. lies ascribed to the Prophet (ﷺ).

[85] *Tafsīr al-Ṭabarī*, vol. 4, pp. 628-629.

This also includes what is narrated regarding the verse:

وَلِكُلِّ قَوْمٍ هَادٍ

...and for every people is a guide.
Sūrah al-Raʿd, 13:7

Some state that it refers to ʿAlī.

وَتَعِيَهَآ أُذُنٌ وَٰعِيَةٌ ﴿١٢﴾

...and [that] a conscious ear would be conscious of it.
Sūrah al-Ḥāqqah, 69:12

It has also been said that this also refers to ʿAlī.

It seems that this is the explanation given by the *Rāfiḍah*, for they are the ones who normally concoct such notions. There is no doubt that every nation has a guide, but it is not just ʿAlī. Allāh has made it easy for each nation to have a guide, and at the head of them are the Messengers. ***"...And [that] a conscious ear would be conscious of it,"*** includes every ear which harkens and understands what is being said.

A similar narration [to that which the author has mentioned] is what is reported by Ibn Jarīr, Ibn Mardawayh and Abū Nuʿaym from the narration of Ibn ʿAbbās, that when the verse ***"Indeed, you are only a warner and for every people is a guide,"*** was revealed, the Prophet (ﷺ) placed his hand on his chest and said: 'I am the warner.' He then pointed to ʿAlī and said: 'You are the guide O ʿAlī; those guided will be guided through you.'[86] Ibn Kathīr said: 'This *ḥadīth* contains grave errors in it.'[87]

---

[86] *Tafsīr al-Ṭabarī.*

[87] *Tafsīr Ibn Kathīr*, vol. 2, p. 550.

Chapter 5

The Second Category: Differences in *Tafsīr* Relating to Reasoning and Deductions

The second of the two categories in which differences occur relates to reasoning and deduction as opposed to narrations. Most mistakes which occur in *tafsīr* are as a result of two things which appeared after the generation of the companions, their students (*tābiʿūn*) and those who followed them in righteousness. For this reason, you will not find any of these two things in the exegesis and commentaries of those noble scholars, the likes of ʿAbdul-Razzāq,[88] Wakīʿ,[89] ʿAbd ibn Ḥumayd,[90] ʿAbdul-Raḥmān ibn Ibrāhīm Duḥaym, Imām Aḥmad, Isḥāq ibn Rāḥawayh,[91] Baqī

[88] He was ʿAbdul-Razzāq ibn Hamām ibn Nāfiʿ al-Ḥumayrī al-Ṣanʿānī, one of the great scholars and memorizers. He studied under Ibn Jurayj, Hishām ibn Ḥassān, Thawr ibn Yazīd, Maʿmar and Mālik. His students included many noteworthy scholars who would travel to study with him. He was born in the year 126 AH and died in the year 211 AH.

[89] Wakīʿ ibn al-Jarrāḥ ibn Mulayḥ al-Kūfī, a great scholar and student of Hishām ibn ʿUrwah, Ibn ʿAwn and Shuʿbah. He was from the teachers of Imām Aḥmad who said concerning him: 'I have not seen his likes in knowledge, memorization and accuracy; on top of that he possessed piety and god-fearingness.' He died in the year 196 AH.

[90] ʿAbd ibn Ḥumayd ibn Naṣr al-Kassī, from the teachers of Muslim and al-Tirmidhī. Ibn Ḥajar said in *Taqrīb*: 'A trustworthy memorizer.' He passed away in the year 249 AH.

[91] Abū Muḥammad Isḥāq ibn Ibrāhīm al-Rāḥawayh, died 238 AH. He was the most outstanding scholar of *ḥadīth* and *fiqh* in Khurasān during his time.

ibn Mukhlid,[92] Abū Bakr ibn al-Mundhir, Sufyān ibn 'Uyaynah,[93] Sunayd, Ibn Jarīr,[94] Ibn Abī Ḥātim,[95] Abū Sa'īd al-Ashajj, Abū 'Abdullāh ibn Mājah[96] and Ibn Mardawayh.

The first problem which arose was people believing in certain ideologies and then interpreting the Qur'ān to fit those ideologies. The second problem was a group of people who interpreted the Qur'ān just as an average Arabic speaker would, without considering from whom these words came, to whom it was revealed and who they were addressing.

Therefore, the first group of people held certain beliefs and ideologies, and then wanted to use the words of the Qur'ān to support their ideologies. This was in both issues of belief as well as in practical rulings. As such, you will find a person who holds a certain belief, trying to change the meanings of the divine texts in order to support his views, whether this is regarding the names and attributes of Allāh, matters of *tawḥīd* or other similar matters.

For example a person will say, 'In my opinion, it is allowed for one to seek closeness to Allāh (*tawassul*) even via the *jinn* and devils. The proof for this is the verse: ***"O you who believe! Fear Allāh and seek the means [of nearness] to Him"***[97] so I may seek

---

[92] Abū 'Abdul-Raḥmān Baqī, a Spanish scholar who died in 276 AH. He was born in Cordoba and travelled to Makkah, Madinah, Egypt, Syria and Iraq.

[93] Sufyān ibn 'Uyaynah ibn Maymūn, died 198 AH. He was born in Kūfah but later settled in Makkah. He was a well-known transmitter of *ḥadīth*.

[94] Abū Ja'far Muḥammad ibn Jarīr al-Ṭabarī, died 310 AH. He was a great historian, an eminent jursist and an outstanding commentator of the Qur'ān. He was born in Tabristan and later settled in Baghdad where he died.

[95] 'Abdul-Raḥmān ibn Abū Ḥātim al-Rāzī, died 327 AH. He was a scholar and critic of *ḥadīth* who penned many works.

[96] Muḥammad ibn Yazīd ibn Mājah, died 273 AH. He is the compiler of the sixth most authentic collection of *ḥadīth*.

[97] Sūrah al-Mā'idah, 5:35.

nearness to Him by any means necessary.' Similarly, he may deny the attributes of Allāh using as evidence the verse: ***"There is nothing like unto Him"***[98] claiming that by affirming an attribute he has inadvertently likened Allāh to His creation. By holding such views that individual then interprets the Qur'ān to support those views.

The second group of people did not possess any preconceived views, rather they interpreted the Qur'ān literally, without considering from whom these words originated; Allāh, or to whom they were revealed; the Prophet (ﷺ), or who they were addressing; the ones to whom the Prophet (ﷺ) was sent. They only saw the Qur'ān in a very literal way; this is also incorrect. Everyone agrees that speech can vary in meaning depending upon who is speaking and to whom his words are being addressed.

An example of this is that if a nobleman was to identify a fault in you, and the same fault was also identified by a person of very low social standing, the criticism of the former would have a greater impact than the criticism of the latter. Even though both identified the same fault, the words of a nobleman hold greater weight. Another example of this is if you were to say to someone: 'I swear you are a small man.' This statement would be deemed as praise if the one being addressed is a boy. At the same time, the statement would be dispraise to a fully grown and intellectual man. Therefore, words hold different connotations depending on who one is addressing. Certain people only interpret the meanings of the Qur'ān and *ḥadīth* literally without taking into account the speaker, audience and other similar factors.

[98] Sūrah al-Shūrā, 42:11.

The first group concentrated on meanings that suited them without paying any attention to the real implications and contexts of the verses. The second group concentrated on the words and how they were used by the Arabs and disregarded the context of the verses. This group also mistakenly interprets words of the Arabic language thinking that their interpretations are linguistically correct. The first group also falls into this error, but more so [their error is that] as they are incorrect in the interpretations they give to the meanings of the Qur'ān; the other group is also guilty of this. The first group prefers to concentrate on meanings and the other group places emphasis on words.

It is obligatory upon a person that when he looks at a word he also considers the different contexts attached to that word, such as the speaker and the audience etc. This is something well known as even ones facial expressions can have an impact. A person who speaks with a harsh tone, redness in his eyes, puffed cheeks and a temper is not similar to one who speaks with calmness and gentleness. The first throws off sparks whilst the second does not.

Here, the author (may Allāh have mercy upon him) has mentioned two categories of people. A group who consider the meanings but twist them to support their own beliefs, and a group with no preconceived notions, who take the literal meaning of the word irrespective of the context of the words.

The first group is further divided into two sub-groups; a group which strips the words of the Qur'ān of their real and intended meaning, and a group which gives the words meanings which they do not convey. In both instances, that which they wish to affirm or negate may be incorrect and therefore they have erred in both the evidence and the ideology they wish to support with it, or that particular idea may be correct in which case they have only erred in the way they use the evidence. Just as this method is present in the exegesis of the Qur'ān, it is also present in the exegesis of *ḥadīth*.

Those who err in both the evidence and the ideology such as the sects of the people of innovation oppose the truth which the moderate *Ummah* holds onto; they are those who do not agree upon misguidance such as the predecessors of this nation.

They interpret the Qur'ān and twist it to support their views. At times they use verses as evidence even though these verses do not support them, and at times they twist and change that which contradicts their views, thus distorting these words from their proper usages.

The difference between using verses as evidence, even though those verses do not support particular views and explaining away verses which contradict those views can better be highlighted by use of an example. The Muʿaṭṭilah state regarding the verse ***"There is nothing like unto Him"*** that 'this implies that we do not affirm for Allāh any attribute which the creation possesses.' This statement of theirs is incorrect and the verse does not support this view. Sometimes this group may distort the meanings of words and say, '[Allāh's] hand means power or blessing' so even though they affirm the attribute they distort its meaning. Therefore, they either give words meanings they don't convey or explain away meanings they do convey.

A further example of this is what is prevalent in our times. It includes those who interpret the Qur'ān with what they refer to as miraculous wonders of the Qur'ān, for sometimes they too interpret the Qur'ān incorrectly. It is true that these people have made many good deductions which attest to the truthfulness of the Qur'ān and that it is from Allāh. This is especially beneficial for *da'wah* to non-Muslims who rely upon intellectual evidences and what they can sense in order to establish the truthfulness of what the Messenger (ﷺ) came with. However, at times they interpret the words of the Qur'ān with meanings those words do not convey. For example, the verse, ***"O company of jinn and mankind, if you are able to pass beyond the regions of the heavens and the earth, then pass. You will not pass except by authority [from Allāh]."***[99] They claim these verses predict the landing on the moon and other planets, for they interpret 'authority' in this verse to mean 'knowledge'. This is without a doubt distortion, and it is *ḥarām* to give such an interpretation. One who contemplates over the verse will realise that it is discussing the Day of Judgement, and the context in which this verse comes supports this. Allāh says, ***"If you are able to pass beyond the regions of the heavens and the earth, then pass."*** These people have not even reached the heavens, let alone pass beyond them. The next verse then states, ***"There will be sent upon you a flame of fire and smoke"*** – no such thing happens to astronauts.

The point being made here is there are people who go to extremes in trying to prove matters using the Qur'ān which the verses do not support, and there are others who deny what the Qur'ān supports. If the Qur'ān supports recent discoveries then one can explain the words of the Qur'ān as such. This is only if the words convey that meaning, otherwise one must avoid conveying meanings which do not exist.

[99] Sūrah al-Raḥmān, 55:33.

From these groups are the Khawārij,[100] Rawāfiḍ, Jaḥmiyyah,[101] Muʿtazilah,[102] Qadariyyah[103], Murji'ah[104] and others. From amongst them the Muʿtazilah are especially known for their rhetoric and argumentation.

The Khawārij take the verses of punishment and what apparently refers to disbelief, and say that a Muslim becomes a disbeliever by committing a major sin. The Rāfiḍah distort the Qur'ān and will say that the verse: ***"He released the two seas, meeting [side by side]"***[105] refers to Fāṭimah. They also state that the verse ***"as was the accursed tree [mentioned] in the Qur'ān"***[106] refers to *Banū Umayyah*. They have many such evil interpretations – we seek refuge from Allāh – they distort the words of the Qur'ān which dispraise and use them against their opponents, and then distort the verses of praise and use them for those they support.

Likewise, the Jaḥmiyyah, the followers of Jaḥm ibn Ṣafwān, distort all the verses pertaining to the attributes of Allāh. They

[100] Originally the Khawārij are those who left the camp of ʿAlī after he agreed to arbitration between himself and Muʿāwiyah after the Battle of Ṣiffīn. They condemned arbitration as an act of disbelief. Later, they held that all who committed major sins were disbelievers. Many of their sub-sects have now disappeared although some remnants still remain.

[101] The Jaḥmiyyah are the followers of Jaḥm ibn Ṣafwān who was executed by Ibn ʿAjwān al-Muzanī in 123 AH. They believe that man has no free will and that faith only comprises of the knowledge of Allāh and no action. Among their beliefs is that the Qur'ān is created.

[102] Muʿtazilah is the name given to Wāṣil ibn ʿAṭā' and others who followed him when he left his teacher al-Ḥasan al-Baṣrī. He left over the issue regarding the position of the one who commits a major sin. Wāṣil held that he was neither a Muslim nor a disbeliever, instead he was in a position between the two.

[103] Qadariyyah are those who deny the pre-decree of Allāh and His creation of human actions. Instead, they assert that man is completely free in his will and choice and as such is the creator of his own actions.

[104] The Murji'ah are the extreme opponents of the Khawārij. They believe that faith is mere knowledge and that it is not lost through sin, no matter how grave the sin may be. As for whether or not such a person will be punished in the Hereafter, this is left to the Will of Allāh.

[105] Sūrah al-Raḥmān, 55:19.

[106] Sūrah al-Isrā', 17:60.

believe that Allāh possesses no attributes and that His names are void of meaning. Yet others from them claim that Allāh has neither names nor attributes, and that these names refer to His creation. However we praise Allāh for He states in the Qur'ān, ***"and Allāh guided those who believed to the truth concerning that over which they had differed."***[107]

The Mu'tazilah are the followers of Wāṣil ibn 'Aṭā' and 'Amr ibn 'Ubayd, and as Shaykh al-Islām describes them; are known for their excessive rhetoric. This is because they constantly refer to the intellect and give no weight to religious texts, even in matters which the intellect does not comprehend. Their principle concerning the attributes of Allāh is that which is affirmed by intellect is real, irrespective of whether or not it is supported by the Qur'ān and *Sunnah*. Similarly, that which is negated by intellect is denied whether or not it is present in the Qur'ān and *Sunnah*. As for that which is neither affirmed nor negated by intellect, most of them deny it claiming that they only affirm what is affirmed by intellect. Others do not pass judgement on this last category as intellect neither supports nor negates it. In all of this they go to extreme lengths in producing arguments and rhetoric. You would be amazed at the lengths they go to, although their arguments are futile. They contradict one another. You will find that one asserts that Allāh must be described with such and such an attribute, while another argues it is impossible for Allāh to be described with that attribute. These contradictory statements are sufficient in depicting their futility.

[107] Sūrah al-Baqarah, 2:213

They have authored commentaries of the Qur'ān based upon their beliefs and principles, such as the *tafsīr* of ʿAbdul-Raḥmān ibn Kaysān al-Aṣamm, the teacher of Ibrāhīm ibn Ismāʿīl ibn ʿUlayyah who used to debate with al-Shāfiʿī. Likewise there is the book of Abū ʿAlī al-Jubbā'ī,[108] *Tafsīr al-Kabīr* by Qāḍī ʿAbdul-Jabbār ibn Aḥmad al-Ḥamdānī,[109] *al-Jāmi' li-'Ilm al-Qur'ān* by ʿAlī ibn ʿĪsā al-Rummānī, and *al-Kashāf* by Abul-Qāsim al-Zamakhsharī. All of these authors and others like them held the beliefs of the Muʿtazilah.

Al-Kashāf by Abul-Qāsim az-Zamakhsharī is a famous and widely available book. It excels in terms of language and eloquence, but as the author mentions it conforms to the beliefs of the Muʿtazilah. However, the only person who will be able to discern this is one who has knowledge of their beliefs and the beliefs of Ahlus-Sunnah. This is due to the author's eloquence and style; he will mention something which will seem correct when in reality it is the opposite. For example in the verse, ***"So he who is drawn away from the Fire and admitted to Paradise has attained [his desire]."***[110] He comments, 'Which success is greater than entering Paradise and being saved from the Fire?' This is a good statement, however what is intended by it is to deny that the believers will see Allāh in the Hereafter; this is the greatest of rewards as Allāh says, ***"For them who have done good is the best [reward] – and extra."***[111] If a person was to read al-Zamakhsharī's words he would think they were correct, as there is no greater reward than entering Paradise and being saved from the Fire. However one will not realise that he is denying the seeing of Allāh, for this is the greatest reward and is greater

[108] Abū ʿAlī Muḥammad ibn ʿAbdul-Wahhāb al-Jubbā'ī, died 303 AH. He was one of the leaders of the Muʿtazilah and is also credited with a commentary on the Qur'ān.

[109] Qāḍī ʿAbdul-Jabbār ibn Aḥmad al-Ḥamdānī, died 415 AH. He was an eminent Muʿtazilī writer, theologian and judge who wrote many works.

[110] Sūrah l-ʿImrān, 3:185.

[111] Sūrah Yūnus, 10:26.

than entering Paradise. As such, al-Zamakhsharī has statements of this nature in which he plays with the minds. If one is not aware of this, and is unfamiliar with the beliefs of the Muʿtazilah and the beliefs of Ahlus-Sunnah then he will be misguided. This is in relation to his commentary on the names and attributes of Allāh and other beliefs they hold. His comments on language and eloquence however are good.

The principles of the Muʿtazilah are five: *tawḥīd*, justice, the station between two stations, implementation of the punishment and ordering the good and forbidding the evil. Their concept of *tawḥīd* is similar to that of the Jaḥmiyyah's, i.e. denying the attributes of Allāh.

They claim that from their principles is *tawḥīd* (oneness of Allāh), however their concept of *tawḥīd* is different. Another principle is justice, which is also a great principle as Allāh says,

إِنَّ ٱللَّهَ يَأْمُرُ بِٱلْعَدْلِ وَٱلْإِحْسَـٰنِ

Indeed, Allāh orders justice and good conduct
Sūrah al-Naḥl, 16:90

The third principle is the station between two stations. In order to understand what they mean by this we will put forth an example: There is a man who performs all his religious duties and refrains from sins, another who is a believer who has committed major sins and a third who is a disbeliever. Are all three equal in station? They claim that the believer who committed major sins is in a station between the other two stations, i.e. neither a believer nor a disbeliever.

The fourth principle is implementation of punishments. They argue that Allāh has ordained punishments for certain sins which do not amount to disbelief. For example, Allāh says,

وَمَن يَقْتُلْ مُؤْمِنًا مُّتَعَمِّدًا فَجَزَآؤُهُۥ جَهَنَّمُ
خَـٰلِدًا فِيهَا وَغَضِبَ ٱللَّهُ عَلَيْهِ وَلَعَنَهُۥ وَأَعَدَّ لَهُۥ
عَذَابًا عَظِيمًا ﴿٩٣﴾

But whoever kills a believer intentionally – his recompense is Hell, wherein he will abide eternally, and Allāh has become angry with him and has cursed him and has prepared for him a great punishment.
Sūrah al-Nisā', 4:93

Likewise, included in this is the Prophet's (ﷺ) statement, "*Three people will not enter Paradise: an alcoholic, one who severs his ties of kinship and the one who constantly reminds others of his favours over them,*"[112] and the *ḥadīth*, "*On the Day of Judgement, Allāh will not speak to three types of people, nor will he look at them or purify them and for them is a painful torment: the one whose clothes drag beneath him, the one who constantly reminds others of his favours over them and the one who sells his items by making false oaths.*"[113] The Muʿtazilah say that it is incumbent upon them to implement these punishments. They argue that the one who prescribed these punishments is Allāh who is Able to do all things, so these punishments must be enforced.

The final principle is to order the good and forbid the evil, and what a blessed principle it is. However, we will discuss later the false meanings that they intend by this principle. They deceive people by taking principles which apparently seem noble, but once explained and clarified one realises they are false.

[112] *Sunan al-Nasāʾī*, no. 2562.

[113] *Sahih Muslim*, no. 106.

Their concept of *tawḥīd* is similar to that of the Jaḥmiyyah's, i.e. denying the attributes of Allāh. They claim that Allāh will not be seen, that the Qur'ān is created, and that Allāh is not above His creation. They further claim that He does not possess knowledge, power, life, hearing, sight, speech, will or any other attribute.

Thus, their concept of *tawḥīd* is to negate all of Allāh's attributes from Him. They say that the oneness of Allāh implies to negate His attributes, for if you affirm an attribute for Him then you have compared Him to something else, and He is no longer unique.

Tawḥīd is based upon two matters: negation and affirmation. It signifies uniqueness which is not attained by only negation or affirmation, as negation on its own is to devoid all meaning (*ta'ṭīl*), and affirmation on its own does not rule out others possessing similar attributes, therefore uniqueness can only be achieved by both negation and affirmation.

If one was to say, 'there is no-one standing', this is negation, and as such this position of standing has been negated from everyone, which now makes it devoid of meaning. On the other hand to say, 'Zayd is standing' is affirmation but it does not exclude anyone else from also standing, so others may be participating in this action. However, if you were to say, 'no-one is standing except Zayd', this is *tawḥīd* [linguistically]. Zayd is now unique in this action.

This is the meaning of *lā ilāha ilal Allāh* (none has the right to be worshipped except Allāh). However, they claim that *tawḥīd* is not to affirm an attribute for Allāh – and we seek Allāh's protection – so He does not possess hearing, sight, power, life, knowledge or anything else.

Their concept of justice involves believing that Allāh did not will creation [i.e. that they should exist], create them nor does He possess power over them. They also believe that Allāh doesn't create the actions of His slaves, whether good or bad. He only wants that which He has ordered in his divine laws. All else may take place without his permission.

They assert that Allāh does not will everything which takes place, nor does His will encompass the actions of His servants, nor did He create everything. Their argument for this is that if Allāh gave these actions permission to take place and created them, then He was to punish people for their actions, this would amount to oppression. In contrast, if we said that Allāh does not create these actions, but He punishes people because they perform them, this is justice. If this argument was to be put to the layman, he would probably immediately agree.

However, in response to this argument it is said that in reality this is *ta'ṭīl* and describing the Creator as deficient – this is because it implies that there exists in the universe that which He does not want nor that which He wills, or that He did not create everything which exists, even though Allāh says,

ٱللَّهُ خَٰلِقُ كُلِّ شَيۡءٖۖ

Allāh is the Creator of all things
Sūrah al-Zumar, 39:62

Furthermore we say, the alleged oppression can be refuted in two ways; with intellectual and textual evidence. Intellectually, it can be said that unlike animals, Allāh gave every human being intellect with which he can differentiate between good and bad, and benefit and harm. As for textual evidence, Allāh sent the Messengers who clarified truth and falsehood, and established the evidence:

رُّسُلًا مُّبَشِّرِينَ وَمُنذِرِينَ لِئَلَّا يَكُونَ لِلنَّاسِ عَلَى ٱللَّهِ
حُجَّةٌۢ بَعْدَ ٱلرُّسُلِ

[We sent] messengers as bringers of good tidings and warners so that mankind will have no argument against Allāh after the messengers.

Sūrah al-Nisā', 4:165

Actual oppression would be to say, 'Do as you please', then after you do as you please you are punished. Warning against certain actions and then punishing you for performing them is not oppression. This is similar to a man who warns his son against a particular action, and then reprimands the child when he disobeys his command. The man's actions are considered a means of rectification. Hence, one can see how they [the Muʿtazilah] deceive and debate, and the falsehood they call to. They then state that Allāh only wants that which He orders, so to them His want and order is synonymous. This is also incorrect, for this claim means that the majority of people act in contradiction to Allāh's divine orders, as from every thousand, nine hundred and ninety nine oppose Allāh's legislative orders. As such, there is no doubt that there is a difference between pleasure associated with an order and a will which encompasses that which He ordered and that which He didn't.

Others who agreed with them on this point are the Shīʿah of later times, the likes of al-Mufīd, Abū Jaʿfar al-Ṭūsī and others.

Here, the author (may Allāh have mercy upon him) addresses them as Shīʿah whereas he previously referred to them as Rawāfiḍ. They are Shīʿah in the sense that they claim to be the supporters of ʿAlī ibn Abū Ṭālib. They are Rawāfiḍ because they rejected Zayd ibn ʿAlī ibn al-Ḥusayn when they asked him concerning Abū Bakr and ʿUmar. He replied by praising them and stating that they were the ministers of his great grandfather, i.e. the Prophet (ﷺ). As a result they rejected him and removed him from his position, and henceforth were known as Rāfiḍah.

The reality is that Ahlus-Sunnah are the true supporters of ʿAlī ibn Abū Ṭālib (رضي الله عنه) and the other believing members of the prophetic household. The believers are helpers and supporters of one another. Allāh states:

وَٱلْمُؤْمِنُونَ وَٱلْمُؤْمِنَٰتُ بَعْضُهُمْ أَوْلِيَآءُ بَعْضٍ

The believing men and believing women are allies of one another.

Sūrah al-Tawbah, 9:71

The stronger one's faith in Allāh, the greater his alliance is to the believers of the prophetic household and others. ʿAlī ibn Abū Ṭālib himself is free of the statements which they attribute to him. Rather he burnt those of them who came to him and claimed that he was god – and we seek refuge in Allāh. He was unable to control his anger, so he ordered that ditches be dug, wood be gathered and then ordered they be thrown into this fire due to them claiming he was god. Those who do not verbally claim that he is god often do so in meaning. They believe that he controls the universe and that nothing moves in the heavens or the earth except by the power of ʿAlī.

We ask Allāh to bear witness that the believers love the prophetic household. We also hold that the believing members of that household have certain rights upon us: Firstly, the superiority of their faith, and secondly their relation to the Prophet (ﷺ). They are honoured due to their close relation to the Prophet (ﷺ). The Prophet (ﷺ) is not honoured due to them, but they due to him. They are also of varying levels. Even though they are honoured with this close connection to the Prophet (ﷺ), this does not mean they are more superior to those who excelled them in faith and knowledge. Therefore, Abū Bakr, 'Umar and 'Uthmān are better than 'Alī in terms of general superiority, even though 'Alī may possess some virtues which they do not possess. So there is a difference between general superiority and certain virtues.

As for punishment with fire, 'Alī saw this as the strongest punishment he could inflict upon them, just as Abū Bakr ordered that a homosexual also be burnt. However at times people may not possess complete knowledge of an issue. This is why Ibn 'Abbās said that if he were in the place of 'Alī he would have beheaded them, due to the Prophetic statement: "*Whoever changes his religion then kill him*"[114] and because the Prophet (ﷺ) forbade punishment with the fire.[115] It is said that 'Alī responded to this by saying that the son of Umm Faḍl [Ibn 'Abbās] is not mistaken.

[114] *Sahih al-Bukhāri*, no. 3017.

[115] *Sahih al-Bukhāri*, no. 6922.

Abū Jaʿfar has a *tafsīr* in which he employs the methods of the Muʿtazilah whilst incorporating into that the method of the Twelver Shīʿah's (*Imāmiyyah Ithnā ʿAshriyyah*).[116] The Muʿtazilah do not prescribe to their doctrine and beliefs, nor do they reject the Caliphates of Abū Bakr, ʿUmar, ʿUthman or ʿAlī.

From amongst the principles of the Muʿtazilah and Khawārij is the implementation of punishment. They believe that Allāh will not accept any intercession for those who committed major sins nor will they be removed from the Fire. Without a doubt this belief of theirs has been refuted by some of the Murji'ah, Karāmiyyah[117] and Kalābiyyah[118] and their followers. They often did well in their rebuttal but at times they also erred until the two groups became complete opposites as has been explained elsewhere.

This often occurs; a group of people refute another group who have brought an innovation, but they do this by going to the other extreme and opposing this innovation with another innovation. An example can be given of the day of *ʿĀshūrā'*. Some people now consider it necessary to celebrate this day with joy and happiness, in order to oppose the Rāfiḍah who consider this day one of sadness and grief. However, this is incorrect. It is not allowed to oppose one innovation with another. Rather it is sufficient to simply oppose an innovation by mentioning that it is not from the *sharīʿah*, and that innovations lead to misguidance. Opposing innovations with other innovations will be of no avail, an innovation can only be expelled by a *sunnah*.

[116] The Twelver Shi'ites are those who believe in the infallibility of their twelve imāms. The twelve being, ʿAlī, Ḥasan, Ḥusayn, Zayn al-ʿĀbidīn, Muḥammad al-Bāqir, Jaʿfar al-Ṣādiq, Mūsā al-Kāzim, Riḍā, Muḥammad al-Jawwād, ʿAlī al-Hādī, Ḥasan al-ʿAskarī and finally his son Muḥammad who went into hiding and will be reappearing as the promised *Mahdī* according to them.

[117] The Karāmiyyah are the followers of Abū ʿAbdullāh Muḥammad ibn Karām, died 255 AH. They conceive of Allāh as a substance who is located in space above the Throne. Faith to them is the utterance of the two *shahādahs* which involves neither conviction nor action.

[118] Kalābiyyah are the followers of Abū Muḥammad ʿAbdullāh ibn Saʿid ibn Kullāb al-Qaṭṭān, died 240 AH. They were later absorbed into the Ashʿariyyah.

The point here being that this group of people held certain beliefs and then interpreted the words of the Qur'ān in support of those beliefs. In this regard they have no predecessors from the companions, their students (*tābi'ūn*) or those who followed them from the great scholars of the Muslims, neither in their beliefs nor in their commentaries of the Qur'ān. The faults of their interpretations of the Qur'ān can be seen from many angles. Two main ways are: possessing knowledge of the futility of their views and knowledge of their incorrect interpretations of the Qur'ān, either by refuting their position or by defending the positions they attack.

From amongst them are individuals who are eloquent and charming, and able to conceal their innovations so that most people will not realise their deception. This includes the author of *al-Kashāf* and others. This particular author manages to confuse many who would not expect him to possess erroneous views. I know of many commentators of the Qur'ān and others who freely quote from these people in their works, who even though they do not agree with their views or principles, do not realise the errors in their writings.

This is because these people are proficient in their style and technique. One will think that their apparent words are good and beneficial but within them is concealed poison. Those who quote from their works – even though they disagree with their views, are also deceived by their words and technique which blinds them from noticing their falsehood. We have mentioned that these people hold views and then twist evidences to support them, or use as evidence texts which do not support their views.

Then, due to their extremism in this, groups such as the Rāfiḍah Imāmiyyah, followed by the philosophers and then the Qarāmiṭah and others have gone to even further extremes. The philosophers and Qarāmiṭah have especially exacerbated this issue by interpreting the Qur'ān in the strangest of ways. Examples of commentaries by the Rāfiḍah are:

تَبَّتْ يَدَآ أَبِي لَهَبٍ وَتَبَّ ١

May the hands of Abū Lahab be ruined, and ruined is he

Sūrah al-Masad, 111:1

[They claim that] 'The two hands are Abū Bakr and 'Umar'.

They claim that the two hands of Abū Lahab are Abū Bakr and 'Umar. This exemplifies the reality of the Rāfiḍah, and the enormous hatred and animosity they possess towards the companions (ﷺ). Rather, this hatred extends further to Islām. They openly claim to be Muslims and followers of Islām, whereas in reality they possess the most severe hatred and enmity towards the companions of the Prophet (ﷺ). How can a person claim to be a Muslim, and then say that this verse was revealed concerning Abū Bakr and 'Umar who are the two greatest companions? If verses such as this were revealed concerning these two companions, then the Muslims have no honour left.

لَئِنْ أَشْرَكْتَ لَيَحْبَطَنَّ عَمَلُكَ

...if you should associate [anything] with Allāh, your work would surely become worthless
Sūrah al-Zumar, 39:65

[They interpret this to mean] 'between Abū Bakr and 'Umar vis a vis 'Alī in terms of the caliphate'.

The actual meaning of the verse refers to associating partners with Allāh. The claim of the Rāfiḍah is that it refers to who should be the caliph amongst these three, i.e. if you make them leaders [instead of 'Alī] then your actions will be rendered null and void. Here, we can see how they have completely distorted the meaning of the Qur'ān to the most extreme lengths, and we seek refuge in Allāh.

إِنَّ ٱللَّهَ يَأْمُرُكُمْ أَن تَذْبَحُوا۟ بَقَرَةً

"Indeed, Allāh commands you to slaughter a cow."
Sūrah al-Baqarah, 2:67

'The cow to be slaughtered is referring to 'Ā'ishah' according to them.

May Allāh destroy them. This statement is from Mūsā to his people. However, they assert that it is 'Ā'ishah who is being referred to, and that Allāh ordered us to slaughter her. In my personal opinion, anyone who makes such wild interpretations has committed an act of disbelief – and we seek refuge in Allāh. Without a doubt these people possess no shame, not from Allāh or the servants of Allāh. ***"And [recall] when Moses said to his people, 'Indeed, Allāh commands you to slaughter a cow.'"*** What relation does 'Ā'ishah have to Mūsā that it would warrant the revelation of such a verse.

This is the opinion of the earlier and the later Rāfiḍah, for the latter take from the former. It is incorrect to think that the earlier Rāfiḍah accepted the leadership of Abū Bakr and 'Umar. I have seen the strangest of statements from some, but not all of them; they claim that Abū Bakr, 'Umar, 'Uthmān and 'Alī were all disbelievers. The first three disbelieved due to their oppression and injustice and 'Alī disbelieved because he did not defend the truth and allowed falsehood to prevail.

فَقَٰتِلُوٓاْ أَئِمَّةَ ٱلۡكُفۡرِ

...then fight the leaders of disbelief
Sūrah al-Tawbah, 9:12

'The leaders of disbelief are Ṭalḥah and Zubayr', [according to the Rāfiḍah].

This does not make sense. Allāh states: ***"And if they break their oaths after their treaty and defame your religion, then fight the leaders of disbelief."*** This verse speaks about those who had a pact and treaty with the Prophet (ﷺ). The verse can also be applied to others who are similar to them by way of analogy. The verse does not refer to what these people insinuate – and we seek refuge in Allāh, but they are a shameless people.

مَرَجَ ٱلْبَحْرَيْنِ يَلْتَقِيَانِ ﴿١٩﴾

He released the two seas meeting [side by side]
Sūrah al-Raḥmān, 55:19

[This verse is interpreted as] 'The two seas are 'Alī and Fāṭimah'.

ٱللُّؤْلُؤُ وَٱلْمَرْجَانُ ﴿٢٢﴾

...pearl and coral
Sūrah al-Raḥmān, 55:22

'They are Ḥasan and Ḥusayn'.

"He released the two seas meeting [side by side]. Between them is a barrier [so] neither of them transgresses. So which of the favours of your Lord would you deny? From both of them emerge pearl and coral." If there is a barrier between the two seas, does this also mean that there is a barrier between 'Alī and Fāṭimah? This is an absurd commentary, but as the author mentioned, we see the strangest of things due to their evil intentions and poor understanding. Their commentaries comprise these two aspects: evil intent and poor understanding.

The two seas being referred to here, as mentioned by the scholars of exegesis, are the fresh and salt waters. It is said that the barrier between them is what is seen at the mouth of a river where it meets the sea. The current of a river will be powerful but it is as if there is a barrier which stops the river merging with the sea. Others from the scholars have stated that the barrier between the two seas is the dry earth. This shows the power of Allāh as the earth is a globe, and Allāh has withheld the sea so that it does not spill over onto the land. Yet others have said that it is a fine barrier between two oceans, to the extent that fish can differentiate between the two types of water causing certain fish to reside in one and not the other. This shows that the water of two seas is different even if they touch one another.

These are three statements regarding this verse. None of the past or present scholars have ever stated that the two seas represent ʿAlī and Fāṭimah; this is only from the distortions of the Rāfiḍah.

وَكُلَّ شَىْءٍ أَحْصَيْنَٰهُ فِىٓ إِمَامٍ مُّبِينٍ ﴿١٢﴾

...and all things We have enumerated in a clear register
Sūrah Yā Sīn, 36:12

'The register is 'Alī ibn Abū Ṭālib'.

How can one draw such a conclusion from this verse? The register refers to a book which is complete; it witnesses and records all of a person's actions. How can this refer to 'Alī? They claim that this clear register is 'Alī who supports and champions the truth, so Allāh enumerated everything in this man. This is also a clear claim that 'Alī knows the unseen. They further insinuate that 'Alī has the same knowledge of the seen and unseen as Allāh does. Everything which Allāh has enumerated is present within 'Alī ibn Abū Ṭālib.

عَمَّ يَتَسَآءَلُونَ ۝١ عَنِ ٱلنَّبَإِ ٱلْعَظِيمِ ۝٢

About what are they asking one another? About the great news

Sūrah al-Naba', 78:1-2

'The great news is 'Alī ibn Abū Ṭālib'.

"About what are they asking one another? About the great news. That over which they are in disagreement." They state that this refers to 'Alī as people are in disagreement over him. He is praised, dispraised, loved and hated. However, is 'Alī the news or the one the news is about? Furthermore, the verse states that the disagreement is taking place, and not that it will take place in the future, however when this verse was revealed no disagreement was present concerning 'Alī.

إِنَّمَا وَلِيُّكُمُ ٱللَّهُ وَرَسُولُهُۥ وَٱلَّذِينَ ءَامَنُوا۟ ٱلَّذِينَ يُقِيمُونَ ٱلصَّلَوٰةَ وَيُؤْتُونَ ٱلزَّكَوٰةَ وَهُمْ رَٰكِعُونَ ﴿٥٥﴾

Your ally is none but Allāh and [therefore] His Messenger and those who have believed – those who establish prayer and give zakāh, and they bow [in worship].

Sūrah al-Mā'idah, 5:55

The verse is addressing ʿAlī. They then mention a *ḥadīth* which has been classed as fabricated by the agreement of the scholars, in which ʿAlī gave his ring in charity whilst praying.

This is an incorrect interpretation. ***"Your ally is none but Allāh and [therefore] His Messenger and those who have believed"*** – this verse is addressing every believer for each one is an ally to Allāh and His Messenger. Allāh says: ***"Allāh is the ally of those who believe."***[119] The Prophet (ﷺ) said: *"I am closer to the Muslims than themselves."*[120] This is true alliance, and without a doubt ʿAlī ibn Abū Ṭālib is included in this verse, as he was from amongst those who prayed, gave *zakāh*, bowed and prostrated – may Allāh be pleased with him. However, it is not possible to declare that this verse refers to him specifically and no-one else. ʿAlī is included in this verse, just as Abū Bakr, ʿUmar, ʿUthmān, Ibn Masʿūd, Ibn ʿAbbās, Khālid ibn Walīd and others from the companions are also included.

The Prophet (ﷺ) said concerning Zubayr: *"Indeed, every Prophet has a disciple, and indeed my disciple is Zubayr."*[121] Despite this, they allege that Zubayr was from the leaders of disbelief. How is it possible that the disciple of the Messenger (ﷺ) or his closest companions are the leaders of disbelief? What would you think

---

[119] Sūrah al-Baqarah, 2:257.

[120] *Sahih al-Bukhāri*, no. 5371 and *Sahih Muslim*, no. 867.

[121] *Sahih al-Bukhāri*, no. 2846 and *Sahih Muslim*, no. 2415.

of a man whose closest companions are leaders of disbelief? Such a man would be like them, either directly or indirectly, as is stated in the *ḥadīth* which has doubts [regarding its authenticity]: *"A man is upon the religion of his closest friend, so let each one of you choose wisely his closest friend."*[122]

[122] *Sunan al-Tirmidhī*, no. 2378, Imām al-Tirmidhī declared it to be authentic.

أُوْلَٰٓئِكَ عَلَيۡهِمۡ صَلَوَٰتٞ مِّن رَّبِّهِمۡ وَرَحۡمَةٞۖ

Those are the ones upon whom are blessings from their Lord and mercy.

Sūrah al-Baqarah, 2:157

'This verse was revealed concerning 'Alī when Ḥamzah was martyred'.

Glorified be Allāh! Who was more affected by the death of Ḥamzah, 'Alī or the Prophet (ﷺ)? It was the Prophet (ﷺ). Yet they say that 'Alī was more affected and as a result this verse was revealed because of him. Their lies and fabrications have led them to state that 'Alī was more grieved by the death of Ḥamzah than the Prophet (ﷺ). This is – by Allāh – a lie, for no-one was more deeply affected by this than the Prophet (ﷺ).

Similar to these above commentaries is what other commentators mention. An example is the commentary of the following verses:

ٱلصَّٰبِرِينَ وَٱلصَّٰدِقِينَ وَٱلْقَٰنِتِينَ وَٱلْمُنفِقِينَ وَٱلْمُسْتَغْفِرِينَ بِٱلْأَسْحَارِ ﴿١٧﴾

The patient, the true, the obedient, those who spend [in the way of Allāh], and those who seek forgiveness before dawn.
Sūrah Āl-ʿImrān, 3:17

They state that the patient one is the Prophet (ﷺ). The truthful one refers to Abū Bakr, ʿUmar is the obedient one, the one who gives in charity is ʿUthmān and ʿAlī is the seeker of forgiveness.

This is ignorance as all of these attributes can be used to describe a single person. To distribute these characteristics is incorrect. From the descriptions mentioned in the above verse, the obedient seems to be the most noble, so how is it that the Prophet (ﷺ) has the virtue of patience, whilst others possess truthfulness and obedience? The Prophet (ﷺ) was the best in all of these characteristics, the most patient, truthful, obedient and generous to the extent that he would spend without fear of poverty,[123] and sleep on an empty stomach.[124] His seeking forgiveness from Allāh was something truly amazing, he would repent a hundred times in a single day[125] and stand the night in prayer until his feet would swell saying: "*Should I not be a thankful slave?*"[126]

[123] See *Sahih Muslim*, no. 2312.

[124] See *Sunan al-Tirmidhī*, no. 2360 and *Sunan Ibn Mājah*, no. 3347.

[125] See *Sahih Muslim*, no. 2702.

[126] *Sahih al-Bukhāri*, no. 4836 and *Sahih Muslim*, no. 2819.

مُّحَمَّدٌ رَّسُولُ ٱللَّهِ وَٱلَّذِينَ مَعَهُۥٓ

Muhammad is the Messenger of Allāh; and those with him...

i.e. Abū Bakr,

أَشِدَّآءُ عَلَى ٱلْكُفَّارِ

...are forceful against the disbelievers...

meaning ʿUmar,

رُحَمَآءُ بَيْنَهُمْ

...merciful among themselves.

This refers to ʿUthmān.

تَرَىٰهُمْ رُكَّعًا سُجَّدًا

You see them bowing and prostrating [in prayer]

Sūrah al-Fatḥ, 48:29

This is ʿAlī.

The distribution of characteristics in this verse is not from the commentaries of the Rāfiḍah, but it is without doubt deficient. They have arrived at these conclusions because Abū Bakr was present with the Prophet (ﷺ) in the cave, ***"...and he [Muḥammad] said to his companion, "Do not grieve, indeed Allāh is with us."***[127] ʿUmar was the forceful one due to him being the most severe in those matters. ʿUthmān was famous for his kindness, mercy and compassion and ʿAlī was from amongst those who worshipped Allāh much. However, ʿUthmān was also known for his worship, as he would spend much of the night in prayer. Therefore, this interpretation is incorrect. ***"...those with him..."*** i.e. the Prophet (ﷺ) includes all the companions; they are all forceful against the disbelievers and merciful to one another whilst constantly being in the worship of Allāh.

[127] Sūrah al-Tawbah, 9:40.

Even stranger is the commentary of the verse:

وَٱلتِّينِ وَٱلزَّيْتُونِ ﴿١﴾ وَطُورِ سِينِينَ ﴿٢﴾ وَهَٰذَا ٱلْبَلَدِ ٱلْأَمِينِ ﴿٣﴾

By the fig and the olive. And [by] Mount Sinai. And [by] this secure city [i.e. Makkah]

Sūrah al-Tīn, 95:1-3

They comment that the fig is Abū Bakr, ʿUmar is the olive, Mount Sinai is ʿUthmān and ʿAlī is the secure city.

Since this is a book about *tafsīr*, the author is quoting from different works of *tafsīr*. According to this commentary, Abū Bakr is the fig, ʿUmar the olive, ʿUthmān is Mount Sinai and ʿAlī is the secure city. Each of these illustrious companions is described as either edible or habitable – we seek Allāh's protection. The reason for this interpretation may be that since Allāh began with the fig before the olive, the fig must be better, and since Abū Bakr was the first leader he must be the fig, so the order in the verses is relative to the order of the caliphate. Therefore four objects match four names.

These types of distortion are brought from words which in no way imply the said meanings. These words do not specifically refer to certain individuals. Allāh's statement, *"...and those with him are forceful against the disbelievers, merciful among themselves. You see them bowing and prostrating [in prayer]."* These are all descriptions for those with the Prophet; this is what the grammarians refer to as successive predication. All of these adjectives describe those with him, and each description does not connote a particular individual. At times these distortions in exegesis cause what is general to be confined to a specific person, such as the verse, ***"Your ally is none but Allāh and [therefore] His Messenger and those who have believed"*** referring specifically to ʿAlī. Another example is that the verse,

وَٱلَّذِى جَآءَ بِٱلصِّدْقِ وَصَدَّقَ بِهِۦٓ

And the one who has brought the truth [i.e. the Prophet (ﷺ)] and [they who] believed in it

Sūrah al-Zumar, 39:33

Some commentators state that this refers specifically to Abū Bakr.

They state that the above verse was revealed concerning Abū Bakr. We have already mentioned that when the scholars say, 'this verse was revealed because of such and such', this means that they are included in the meaning and as such it is one explanation of the verse. Therefore, whoever stated that this verse was revealed concerning Abū Bakr intended that Abū Bakr is amongst those who have believed in the truth brought by the Prophet (ﷺ). Undoubtedly the first and foremost to have believed was the Prophet (ﷺ) himself, as he brought the truth and believed in it. He was the first to attest to his own truthfulness and to the fact that he was a true messenger sent to all of mankind. He was also ordered to proclaim as much,

قُلْ يَـٰٓأَيُّهَا ٱلنَّاسُ إِنِّى رَسُولُ ٱللَّهِ إِلَيْكُمْ جَمِيعًا ٱلَّذِى

Say, [O Muḥammad], "O mankind, indeed I am the Messenger of Allāh to you all

Sūrah al-Aʿrāf, 7:158

The following verse,

لَا يَسْتَوِي مِنكُم مَّنْ أَنفَقَ مِن قَبْلِ ٱلْفَتْحِ وَقَٰتَلَ

Not equal among you are those who spent before the conquest [of Makkah] and fought [and those who did so after it].
Sūrah al-Ḥadīd, 57:10

is also said to refer to Abū Bakr specifically.

If this statement means that this verse refers only to Abū Bakr, this is incorrect. However, if Abū Bakr is only mentioned as an example of those who spent and fought before the conquest then this is a valid example. It is a firmly established principle that a generalisation cannot be specified or confined in its application except with the presence of evidence which supports such a stance. If for example, it is said concerning the verse, ***"Those to whom people said, 'Indeed the people have gathered against you, so fear them,'"*** that the people who have gathered refers to Abū Sufyān as it has been stated then this is possible. Otherwise it is imperative that what is general remains so because to confine or restrict it is to have an incomplete explanation of the verse. Therefore, the commentary must conform to the meanings of the verse. Specifying something general or generalising something specific is not allowed. If we have a text relating to something specific we cannot generalise it. The only exception is by way of analogy if that is applicable.

The *tafsīr* of the likes of Ibn ʿAṭiyyah[128] is closer to the methodology of Ahlus Sunnah and further from innovation compared to the *tafsīr* of Zamakhsharī. However, if Ibn ʿAṭiyyah had sufficed in mentioning the views of the predecessors found in their books it would have been better. He often quotes from the *tafsīr* of Muḥammad ibn Jarīr al-Ṭabarī whose book is from the greatest works of *tafsīr*, but he then leaves quoting all of the sayings which Ibn Jarīr brings from the *salaf*. Instead he relies on opinions of people he considers to be profound scholars who in reality are scholastic theologians possessing principles similar in nature to those which the Muʿtazilah possess, even though they are closer to the *Sunnah* than the Muʿtazilah. It is important that we give credit where it is due, and to know that this *tafsīr* is according to a particular *madhab*.

This statement of the author's shows that he is fair and just, and that the truth, even if it is from the people of innovation must be accepted. If certain people of innovation are closer to the *Sunnah* than others then they should be praised accordingly for this level of closeness. As for rejecting everything they say without differentiation, simply because it comes from a person of innovation, this is incorrect. A person should always declare the truth wherever he is, irrespective of the speaker. This is why men are judged by the truth and the truth is not judged by men. If you judge the truth by men this makes you a blind follower, but if you judge men by the truth, this is justice. Hence the author (may Allāh have mercy upon him) is saying that we give credit where it is due even to the innovators if some are closer to the *Sunnah* than others. We mention that so and so is closer to the *Sunnah* than so and so.

[128] Abū Muḥammad ʿAbdul-Ḥaqq ibn Ghālib ibn ʿAṭiyyah, died 546 AH. He was a man of letters and poetry as well as being a grammarian and judge from Granada, Spain.

Indeed, if the companions, their students and the scholars have an opinion regarding the commentary of a verse, and another group of people interpreted the same verse in a different way based upon their ideals and beliefs which are contrary to the beliefs of the companions and those who followed them, this latter group is in agreement with the Mu'tazilah and innovators in this respect.

In short, whoever diverts away from the methodology of the companions, their students and their commentaries and leans towards what opposes them is wrong in this. Rather he is an innovator in this respect, even though he may be striving to attain the truth and so be forgiven for his errors.

It is important that we draw attention to this matter; whoever diverts away from the methodology of the companions, the successors and their method of commentary has erred. Rather he is an innovator, even though as a result of his striving for the truth he may be forgiven. We describe such an individual as mistaken and an innovator. Every statement in the religion not according to the Book of Allāh, the *Sunnah* of the Prophet (ﷺ), and the way of the companions or their righteous successors is an innovation. The Prophet (ﷺ) said: "*The worst of affairs are the newly invented matters, and every innovation is a misguidance.*"[129] This is also the case in matters of belief. Everything which opposes the way of the companions and their successors is an innovation. However, is such an individual sinful? If he strove to the best of his ability in trying to reach the truth then he is forgiven as the author stated.

Here, we have two points: the first is the actual statement and the second is the one who issued this statement. The statement which opposes the way of the companions and their successors is an innovation. With regards to the speaker, if he tried to the

[129] *Sahīh Muslim*, no. 867.

best of his ability to attain the truth but still fell short then he is forgiven, for Allāh says:

لَا يُكَلِّفُ ٱللَّهُ نَفْسًا إِلَّا وُسْعَهَا ۚ

Allāh does not charge a soul except [with that within] its capacity.

Sūrah al-Baqarah, 2:286

Such a person is forgiven for his mistakes. This is a principle which is almost unanimously agreed upon. Even if there is a difference of opinion regarding some of its finer details, the general principle is established.

One may ask: How is it that someone who differs from the methodology of the companions and their successors is called an innovator, but that due to his striving he is also forgiven for his error? The answer is that he mentioned a statement not previously known from the companions or their righteous successors, so in this respect he has brought an innovation. However, this does not mean that we classify him as an unconditional innovator because of his error in one matter.

Another question which one may have is in respect to verses which may be connected to modern and recent discoveries. There are no textual evidences or statements from the Prophet (ﷺ) regarding these matters, however there are statements present from the companions and scholars commentating on this verse. Is it then allowed for someone to disregard those statements and instead focus on linguistic and scientific deductions from the Qur'ān? Is such a person also considered to be an innovator?

The answer is that if the Qur'ān does actually allude to those matters then the person is not an innovator, and as such this statement does not contradict the statement of any other scholar. If on the other hand, this view opposes the statements of the predecessors then we reject such views. In most instances, the predecessors would not have commented on such discoveries because they were unaware of them. It is however possible that the Qur'ān generally alludes to such points, but it is rare that the Qur'ān would explicitly mention these events, for if it did then the companions would have been the first to have interpreted it as such. Therefore, if the Qur'ān points to such things, it is permissible to use them in the exegesis of verses, otherwise we must refute those statements. For example, the word 'trial' (*fitnah*) has recently been interpreted to mean 'intellectual warfare'. This is correct as the Prophet (ﷺ) informed us, *"trials like a portion of the moonless night; one will awake as a believer but will have disbelieved by night, or be a believer before he sleeps but have succumbed to disbelief by morning."*[130]

[130] *Sahih Muslim*, no. 118.

The point here is to highlight and clarify the methods of verifying knowledge and the methods of identifying the truth. We know that the Qur'ān was recited by the companions, their students and their subsequent successors, and we know that they were more knowledgeable of the meanings and exegesis of the Qur'ān, as well as more aware of the truth brought by the Prophet (ﷺ) [than us]. Therefore, whoever contradicts their statements and uses different explanations is mistaken in both his deduction and in his method.

He is mistaken in his deduction as he has interpreted the verses incorrectly, and he is mistaken in his method as it has caused him to oppose the interpretations of the *salaf*.

Everyone who opposes their statements possesses certain doubts, either intellectual or textual, as has been expounded upon elsewhere.

This statement of the author's – that the opponents [of the truth] possess doubts [which they cast as arguments] – is very true and also has a basis in the Qur'ān. Allāh mentions this in the verse,

هُوَ ٱلَّذِىٓ أَنزَلَ عَلَيْكَ ٱلْكِتَٰبَ مِنْهُ ءَايَٰتٌ مُّحْكَمَٰتٌ هُنَّ أُمُّ ٱلْكِتَٰبِ
وَأُخَرُ مُتَشَٰبِهَٰتٌ ۖ فَأَمَّا ٱلَّذِينَ فِى قُلُوبِهِمْ زَيْغٌ فَيَتَّبِعُونَ مَا تَشَٰبَهَ مِنْهُ

It is He who has sent down to you, [O Muḥammad], the Book, in it are verses [that are] precise – they are the foundation of the Book – and others unspecific. As for those in whose hearts is deviation [from truth], they will follow that of it which is unspecific.

Sūrah Āl-ʿImrān, 3:7

If a proponent of falsehood presented something which had no doubt in it, it would not be accepted from him. Instead, he brings doubtful matters and due to his deviation he does not base the unspecific upon the precise so as to seek clarification. Rather, he seeks to make it all unspecific and doubtful. As the author states, every opponent of the companions and their righteous successors presents doubts with which they hope to cause confusion and disarray.

Here, we wish to highlight the causes of difference in *tafsīr*. One of the greatest causes is innovation and falsehood where proponents of these go to the extent of distorting the words of Allāh, and interpreting the statements of Allāh and His Messenger (ﷺ) incorrectly and twisting their meanings.

In order to counteract this, one must be aware of the opposing view which is the truth. One must also know that their views are opposed by the views of the *salaf*, and that their commentaries are innovations. Furthermore, one should then study in detail the falsehood of their views by using the clear markers of truth laid down by Allāh. This problem is also prevalent amongst those who write about the exegesis of *ḥadīth* just as it is prevalent amongst those who author in the exegesis of the Qur'ān.

Those who err in their deductions and not their methods are like the *Ṣūfīs*, preachers, jurists and others who interpret the Qur'ān with correct ideas but the words of the Qur'ān do not imply such meanings. An example of this is much of what Abū ʿAbdul-Raḥmān al-Sulamī mentions in *Ḥaqā'iq al-Tafsīr*. If the ideas they propagate are also wrong then without doubt this will fall under the first category; mistakes in deduction and methods, since now the meaning they intend is also false.

CHAPTER 6

Exegesis of the Qur'ān with the Qur'ān, and Exegesis with the *Sunnah* and the Statements of the Companions

If one were to ask: What is the best method of *tafsīr*? The response would be that the most authentic of methods is to first explain the Qur'ān with the Qur'ān. This is because what is mentioned briefly in one place will be expounded upon in another place, and what is summarised in one place will be explained in detail elsewhere.

If you are unable to do this then use the *Sunnah* as it is an explanation of the Qur'ān. Imām Abū 'Abdullāh Muḥammad ibn Idrīs al-Shāfi'ī said, 'Every ruling the Prophet (ﷺ) issued was derived from the Qur'ān'. Allāh states,

إِنَّآ أَنزَلۡنَآ إِلَيۡكَ ٱلۡكِتَٰبَ بِٱلۡحَقِّ لِتَحۡكُمَ بَيۡنَ
ٱلنَّاسِ بِمَآ أَرَىٰكَ ٱللَّهُۚ وَلَا تَكُن لِّلۡخَآئِنِينَ خَصِيمٗا ١٠٥

Indeed, We have revealed to you, [O Muḥammad], the Book in truth so you may judge between the people by that which Allāh has shown you. And do not be for the deceitful an advocate.
Sūrah al-Nisā', 4:105

He also says,

وَأَنزَلْنَآ إِلَيْكَ
ٱلذِّكْرَ لِتُبَيِّنَ لِلنَّاسِ مَا نُزِّلَ إِلَيْهِمْ وَلَعَلَّهُمْ يَتَفَكَّرُونَ

And We revealed to you the message [i.e. the Qur'ān] that you may make clear to the people what was sent down to them and that they might give thought.

Sūrah al-Naḥl, 16:44

In yet another verse, He states,

وَمَآ أَنزَلْنَا عَلَيْكَ ٱلْكِتَٰبَ إِلَّا لِتُبَيِّنَ لَهُمُ
ٱلَّذِى ٱخْتَلَفُوا۟ فِيهِ ۙ وَهُدًى وَرَحْمَةً لِّقَوْمٍ يُؤْمِنُونَ ﴿٦٤﴾

And We have not revealed to you the Book, [O Muḥammad], except for you to make clear to them that wherein they have differed and as guidance and mercy for a people who believe.

Sūrah al-Naḥl, 16:64

This is why the Prophet (ﷺ) said, "*Indeed, I have been given the Book and something similar to it*"[131] i.e. the *Sunnah*. The *Sunnah* is also a form of revelation similar to the Qur'ān although it is not recited as the Qur'ān is recited. Imām al-Shāfiʿī and others have quoted many evidences in support of this, however this is not the place to go into detail about that.

The point here is that you seek to understand the Qur'ān with the Qur'ān. After this one goes to the *Sunnah*, as the Prophet (ﷺ) said to Muʿādh ibn Jabal when he sent him to Yemen, "*With what will you judge?" He replied, "With the Book of Allāh." He asked, "And if you do not find [the ruling] in it?" He replied, "Then the Sunnah of the Prophet (ﷺ)" He then asked, "And if you do not find [the ruling] in it?" He replied, "I will use my own judgement." The Prophet (ﷺ) struck his chest and said, "All*

[131] *Sunan Abu Dawud*, no. 4604.

praise is to Allāh who had guided the emissary of the Messenger of Allāh to what pleases the Messenger of Allāh."[132] This *ḥadīth* is found in the books of *Sunan* and its chain of narration is sound.

Some scholars have commented on this *ḥadīth* and classified it as weak, however the author believes its chain of narration to be sound and this seems more likely. This is because it agrees with the general principles of the *sharīʿah*, that one should judge by the Book of Allāh and then with the *Sunnah* of the Prophet (ﷺ), for the *Sunnah* contains that which is not explained in the Qur'ān and so one must refer to it. As for what is not found in the Qur'ān or the *Sunnah*, one uses his judgement. This does not imply that a person follows his own ideas and intellect, but rather that he strives in the application of the principles of the Qur'ān and *Sunnah*. As such, this *ḥadīth* complies with the general principles of the *sharīʿah*. Those who have classified this *ḥadīth* as weak mistakenly think that the statement, 'and if you do not find it in the *Sunnah*' implies that the *Sunnah* has a low status, and that the statement, 'I will use my judgement' implies following one's own intellect.

If one were to ask, does the *Sunnah* abrogate the Qur'ān, the answer would be that if it is authentic then it does, but it is difficult to give a simple example for this. As for the statement of the Prophet (ﷺ), *"There is no bequest for an inheritor,"*[133] it is an incorrect example for this issue. The Prophet (ﷺ) stated, *"Indeed Allāh has given everyone their due right"*,[134] so in this *ḥadīth* it is as if the Prophet (ﷺ) is saying your predetermined shares of the deceased's estate is sufficient, and so you are not entitled to his will.

---

[132] *Sunan Abu Dawud*, no. 3592 and *Sunan al-Tirmidhī*, no. 1327.

[133] *Sahih al-Bukhāri*.

[134] *Sunan Abu Dawud*, no. 3565, *Sunan al-Tirmidhī*, no. 2120 and *Sunan Ibn Mājah*, no. 2713.

If we were to really scrutinise this *ḥadīth* we would find that it does not abrogate the verse in the Qur'ān which states,

كُتِبَ عَلَيۡكُمۡ إِذَا حَضَرَ أَحَدَكُمُ ٱلۡمَوۡتُ إِن تَرَكَ خَيۡرًا
ٱلۡوَصِيَّةُ لِلۡوَٰلِدَيۡنِ وَٱلۡأَقۡرَبِينَ

Prescribed for you when death approaches [any] one of you if he leaves wealth [is that he should make] a bequest for the parents and near relatives.

Sūrah al-Baqarah, 2:180

Hence, this verse has been specified and not abrogated, for the near relatives are not the legal inheritors and so the bequest is still applicable to them. Therefore, the *ḥadīth* only specifies and does not abrogate the verse. As such, this is not an example for abrogation [of the Qur'ān by the *Sunnah*].

Thus, if you do not find the *tafsīr* in the Qur'ān or *Sunnah* you return to the statements of the companions, for they are more knowledgeable regarding this as they witnessed the revelation of the Qur'ān and the circumstances which surrounded its revelation. They also possessed complete understanding along with correct knowledge and righteous action. This is especially the case with their leaders and scholars, like the four rightly guided caliphs and their righteous scholars such as ʿAbdullāh ibn Masʿūd. Imām Abū Jaʿfar Muḥammad ibn Jarīr al-Ṭabarī said: Abū Kurayb narrated to us: Jābir ibn Nūḥ informed us that al-Aʿmash informed him, relating from Abū Ḍuḥā from Masrūq that ʿAbdullāh ibn Masʿūd said, "By the One besides whom there is no other god, not a single verse has been revealed except that I know about whom it was revealed and where it was revealed, and were I to know of anyone more knowledgeable than me in this regard and I was able to reach him then I would travel to him."

This is an example of travelling for the sake of seeking knowledge. It is not the intention of Ibn Masʿūd to lavish praise upon himself or to show-off. Rather his intention is to encourage people to learn the Book of Allāh and its meanings, and to teach them the *tafsīr* of Allāh's words.

A'mash relates from Abū Wā'il that Ibn Mas'ūd said, "When a man from amongst us would learn ten verses he would not proceed until he fully understood their meaning and acted upon them." Also from them [i.e. the scholars of the companions] is the ink and ocean [of this nation] 'Abdullāh ibn 'Abbās, the cousin of the Prophet (ﷺ).

He is known as an ocean due to his vast knowledge. Likewise the term 'ink' also implies extensive knowledge. Both 'ink' and 'ocean' are vast in their nature.

He [i.e. Ibn ʿAbbās] was also known as the interpreter of the Qur'ān due to the blessings of the *duʿā'* the Prophet (ﷺ) made for him, *"O Allāh, give him understanding of the religion and teach him the interpretation [of the Qur'ān]"*.[135]

Ibn Jarīr stated: Muḥammad ibn Bashār narrated to us that he was informed by Wakīʿ who was informed by Sufyān, from the authority of Aʿmash from Muslim who said: ʿAbdullah ibn Masʿūd said: 'What a blessed interpreter of the Qur'ān Ibn ʿAbbās is'. He then quoted another chain of narration from Yaḥyā ibn Dāwūd from Ishāq al-Azraq, on the authority of Sufyān from Aʿmash from Muslim ibn Ṣabīḥ Abū Ḍuḥā, who narrated from Masrūq that Ibn Masʿūd said, 'What a blessed interpreter of the Qur'ān Ibn ʿAbbās is'. A third chain of narration is then mentioned from Bandār, who related from Jaʿfar ibn ʿAwn from Aʿmash that Ibn Masʿūd said the previous about Ibn ʿAbbās. These are authentic chains of narration which all declare that Ibn Masʿūd praised Ibn ʿAbbās using the aforementioned wording. Furthermore, Ibn Masʿūd died in the year 33 AH, and Ibn ʿAbbās lived on for another 36 years, so how much more knowledge would he have acquired during these years? Aʿmash relates from Abū Wā'il that ʿAlī appointed Ibn ʿAbbās leader of the *Ḥajj* season. One day he gave a sermon in which he recited *Sūrah al-Baqarah* – and in a narration – *Sūrah al-Nūr*. He then explained each verse in such a way that were the Romans, Persians and Dalamites to have heard him they would have embraced [Islām].

It is for this reason that the majority of what Ismāʿīl ibn ʿAbdul-Raḥmān al-Suddī the Senior relates in his *tafsīr* is from these two men: Ibn Masʿūd and Ibn ʿAbbās. At times, al-Suddī narrated from them sayings of the People of the Book which the Prophet (ﷺ) allowed in his statement, *"Convey from me even if it is a verse, and there is no harm in narrating from the Children of Israel (Banū Isrā'īl), but whosoever intentionally ascribes lies to*

[135] *Sahih al-Bukhāri*, no. 143 and *Sahih Muslim*, no. 2477.

me will take his place in the Fire."[136] Collected by al-Bukhārī from the *ḥadīth* of ʿAbdullāh ibn ʿAmr.

It is not known that Ibn Masʿūd narrated Israelite traditions; this was more the case with Ibn ʿAbbās. Therefore, I am not sure if the author's statement refers to both of them or just one of them.

[136] *Sahih al-Bukhāri*, no. 3461.

This is why when ʿAbdullāh ibn ʿUmar came into possession of two loads of books belonging to the People of the Book on the Day of Yarmūk, he would narrate from them due to the permissibility stated in the previous *ḥadīth*. However these Israelite traditions are quoted as supporting evidences and not primary sources. These traditions are of three types: a type which is authentic as its truthfulness is attested to by our own sources, a type which is false as our own sources reject it, and a third type which does not fall into the previous two categories, we can neither judge it to be authentic or inauthentic. As such we neither believe in it nor reject it. One is allowed to quote from this third type, even though most of what is contained in it is of no immediate benefit.

The scholars of the People of the Book differ considerably regarding this third category, and as a result the scholars of *tafsīr* quote from them and also differ in this regard. Examples of this category are the names of the companions of the cave, the colour of their dog, and their precise number. Likewise, they differ regarding the type of wood the staff of Mūsā was made from, the types of birds which Allāh gave life to as a sign for Ibrāhīm, which part of the cow was used to strike the slain man, the type of tree Allāh spoke from to Mūsā, and other such matters which are not detailed in the Qur'ān which possess no direct benefit in worldly or religious affairs. However, one may mention the difference of opinion in these matters.

The author states that it is allowed to mention the difference of opinion on such issues. This is not to depend upon their opinions but to clarify the differences of opinion present. It may be that mentioning such differences of opinion from the People of the Book is beneficial for us, as this will cause us to doubt the authenticity of what they quote and to know that they have fabrications and distortions in their narrations. It is impermissible to mention these statements and accept them as truthful unless we have other evidences supporting such views. This is why the author mentioned the three categories of Israelite traditions. We have already mentioned that what we require of knowledge has been mentioned with clear evidences. As for that which is not necessary to know, it may be that there is no proof for it as it is not essential. It is not possible that Allāh would leave His slaves without certain knowledge of what they require with the relevant evidences which show its truthfulness and allow the heart to be content.

Allāh mentions,

سَيَقُولُونَ ثَلَٰثَةٞ
رَّابِعُهُمۡ كَلۡبُهُمۡ وَيَقُولُونَ خَمۡسَةٞ سَادِسُهُمۡ كَلۡبُهُمۡ رَجۡمَۢا
بِٱلۡغَيۡبِۖ وَيَقُولُونَ سَبۡعَةٞ وَثَامِنُهُمۡ كَلۡبُهُمۡۚ قُل رَّبِّيٓ أَعۡلَمُ
بِعِدَّتِهِم مَّا يَعۡلَمُهُمۡ إِلَّا قَلِيلٞۗ فَلَا تُمَارِ فِيهِمۡ إِلَّا مِرَآءٗ ظَٰهِرٗا
وَلَا تَسۡتَفۡتِ فِيهِم مِّنۡهُمۡ أَحَدٗا ٢٢

They [i.e. people] will say there were three, the fourth of them being their dog; and they will say there were five, the sixth of them being their dog – guessing at the unseen; and they will say there were seven, and the eighth of them was their dog. Say, [O Muḥammad], "My Lord is most knowing of their number. None knows them except a few. So do not argue about them except with an obvious argument and do not inquire about them among [the speculators] from anyone."
Sūrah al-Kahf, 18:22

This verse comprises good etiquette in this situation along with teaching what is necessary. Allāh mentions them [i.e. the companions of the cave] in three opinions. He then weakens the first two opinions and remains silent about the third showing its correctness. Were it to also be wrong He would have refuted it as He did the first two. Allāh then states that inquiring about such issues possesses no benefit. As such the befitting response to such an inquiry is, ***"My Lord is most knowing of their number."*** Only a few people know of their exact number as Allāh has given them that knowledge which is why He then says, ***"So do not argue about them except with an obvious argument"*** meaning do not exert your energy in what is unbeneficial. Furthermore, do not ask them concerning such affairs as they only guess the unknown.

This is the best way of mentioning differences of opinion. One gathers all of the relevant opinions, mentions the correct opinion while refuting the incorrect and then states the fruits and benefits derived from the discussion. This is to ensure that one does not prolong discussion over insignificant matters which possess no benefit and one does not digress from what is more crucial and important.

Therefore, the one who does not gather all the different opinions on a particular issue has presented an incomplete argument, as the truth may lie in what he has neglected. Similarly, the one who does not point out the correct opinion has also performed an incomplete task. If one intentionally authenticates something incorrect, he has ascribed lies and falsehood, and if one does this out of ignorance then he has erred.

A person who mentions the varying opinions but does not clarify the correct opinion is blameworthy at times but at other times is free of blame. If one is aware of the truth but does not clarify it, this is deficiency. However if one is unaware [of the correct opinion], for example if two opinions hold equal weight with him, then he is not obliged to choose one over the other. This is also present at times in the works of the author himself, as is found in his *Fatāwā*. He will mention two opinions, then state that one is the opinion of the majority, and the other is the opinion of so and so, or Imām Mālik or al-Shāfiʿī and so on [without choosing].

Therefore, one who mentions issues of difference of opinion must ensure he gathers all the opinions as this is from being trustworthy. Otherwise, as the author mentions, he may neglect a stronger opinion. After this, if he has evidence by which he knows the correct opinion, he must mention this so as not to leave the audience in doubt. On the other hand, if he is unable to choose the correct opinion, there is no harm in just mentioning the opinions without choosing, as Allāh does not burden a soul with more than it can bear.

Similarly, whoever discusses differences in issues which hold little or no benefit, or mentions varying opinions which even though they possess different wordings all dissolve into just one or two opinions has wasted time and has incorrectly exaggerated the matter. Such a person is like one who wears two robes, both of which are stolen. And Allāh guides to the truth.

Concerning the verse the author quoted, some have claimed that [the opinion stating] their number as seven with the eighth being the dog [is also incorrect], as Allāh then states, ***"My Lord is most knowing of their number"***. There is no doubt that this is an incorrect interpretation of this verse, as Allāh mentions this after having refuted the first two opinions and remaining silent on the third, thus showing its correctness. Were this saying to also be incorrect then Allāh would have mentioned this, as Allāh does not agree to what is contrary to the truth. Allāh then states, ***"None knows them except a few"*** and were the statement that Allāh is most knowledgeable regarding them referring to exclusivity then this last statement would be a contradiction. In conclusion, the verse shows that the companions of the cave were seven with the eighth being the dog.

It should also be noted here that Allāh says, ***"...there were seven, and the eighth of them was their dog"*** and He does not refer to them as being eight one of which was a dog. This is because the dog belongs to a different species and as such it is not included in the number but is mentioned after it. This is similar to Allāh's statement,

مَا يَكُونُ مِن نَّجْوَىٰ ثَلَٰثَةٍ إِلَّا هُوَ رَابِعُهُمْ

There is in no private conversation three but that He is the fourth of them
Sūrah al-Mujādilah, 58:7

Again here He does not state that there were four and He is one of them, as He is the Creator and they are the creation.

"So do not argue about them except with an obvious argument". The author explains this part of the verse as meaning, do not exert and tire yourself arguing over the precise number, as there is no benefit in doing so. This also occurs in the field of *ḥadīth*, where at times there are narrations which state, 'a man came' or 'a man said', or 'a Bedouin arrived' etc. You will find many who exert all their efforts into identifying that particular person even though there is no need to do so. As such, these people stress themselves over what may or may not be important, and neglect what is more crucial. Therefore the students of knowledge should not busy themselves with things in which there is little or no benefit.

The conclusion is that the number of the companions of the cave were seven, with the eighth being the dog. We also know that they resided in the cave for three hundred and nine years. Other such [unbeneficial] differences occur regarding the type of wood the staff of Mūsā came from, or the part of the cow used to strike the slain man. All of this is devoid of benefit.

Chapter 7

Exegesis of the Qur'ān with the Statements of the Successors (*Tābiʿūn*)

If one is unable to find the explanation of a verse in the Qur'ān or Sunnah, and does not find any relevant commentaries from the companions, then many of the scholars used the statements of the successors such as Mujāhid ibn Jabr who was a marvel in this science. Muḥammad ibn Isḥāq said that he was informed by Abān ibn Ṣāliḥ that Mujāhid said, 'I recited the whole Qur'ān to Ibn ʿAbbās three times from beginning to end, stopping him at each verse and asking him about it.' Al-Tirmidhī reports from al-Ḥusayn ibn Mahdī al-Baṣrī that ʿAbdul-Razzāq informed him from Maʿmar, who reports from Qatādah that Mujāhid said, 'There is not a single verse in the Qur'ān except I have heard something about it.'[137] Al-Tirmidhī also reports from Abū ʿUmar who narrated from Sufyān ibn ʿUyaynah from Aʿmash that Mujāhid said, 'Had I recited the Qur'ān using the recitation of Ibn Masʿūd, I would not have needed to ask Ibn ʿAbbās about much of what I asked him.'[138] Ibn Jarīr stated: Abū Kurayb informed us from Ṭalaq ibn Ghanām, who related from ʿUthmān al-Makkī from Ibn Abī Mulaykah who said, 'I saw Mujāhid asking Ibn ʿAbbās about the exegesis of the Qur'ān and he had with him his tablets. Ibn ʿAbbās said to him "write" until he went through all

[137] *Sunan al-Tirmidhī*, no. 2952.

[138] Ibid.

of *tafsīr*.' This is why Sufyān al-Thawrī would say, 'If you have the commentary of Mujāhid then it is sufficient.'

Other such successors (*tābiʿūn*) are Saʿīd ibn Jubayr, ʿIkrimah the freed slave of Ibn ʿAbbās, ʿAṭā' ibn Abū Rabāḥ, Ḥasan al-Baṣrī, Masrūq ibn al-Ajdaʿ, Saʿīd ibn al-Musayyib, Abul ʿĀliyah, Rabīʿ ibn Anas, Qatādah, Ḍaḥḥāk ibn Muzāḥim and others from the successors, their students and those who followed them. Their statements are quoted and at times there is a difference in wording, but those who are not grounded in knowledge believe it to be differences of opinion and quote it as such. This is not the case, as some of them mention something by using examples or similes whilst others are explicit in what they are referring to. Most of the time they are in agreement so let the astute be aware of this, and guidance is from Allāh.

Shuʿbah ibn Ḥajjāj and others have said that the statements of the successors in matters such as practical rulings (*aḥkām*) are not authoritative, so how can they be so in issues of *tafsīr*? This means that their opinions are not authoritative over other [successors] who hold contrary views; this is true. However, if they all agree on a single issue then without doubt it is sufficient as evidence. Instead, when they differ, one returns to the language of the Qur'ān or *Sunnah*, or the general Arabic language or statements of the companions.

The shaykh (may Allāh have mercy upon him) mentions the difference of opinion present among the scholars regarding this issue. The author states that 'many of the scholars' allow this [i.e. to use the statements of the successors] but this also shows that there is no consensus on the issue. Furthermore, without doubt there are different levels of successors; those who studied with the companions are not similar to those who did not. Whatever the case, their statements are not sufficient authority over those who opposed their views. This is because they are not from the companions even though their opinions are more likely [than subsequent generations] to be correct. The closer the generation is to the time of the Prophet (ﷺ) the more likely it is that their opinions will be correct. This is obvious as later generations had to battle desires and temptations, and had many generations between them and the era of prophethood. Thus, the later the generation the weaker their knowledge and opinions are. This goes to show the importance of returning to the statements of the *salaf*. As for the deductions of later scholars, this requires more scrutiny as these opinions may be far from the truth.

Hence, the methods for exegesis of the Qur'ān are now four: the Qur'ān, the *Sunnah*, the statements of the companions and the statements of the successors, with a difference of opinion regarding the last category. The author's personal opinion is that if they [i.e. the successors] unite then their statements are sufficient as evidence, but if they differ with one another then they [i.e. their opinions] are not authoritative.

CHAPTER 8

Exegesis of the Qur'ān Based on Intellect and Reason

Exegesis of the Qur'ān based solely on one's reasoning is *ḥarām*. Mu'ammal informed us from the authority of Sufyān from ʿAbdul-Aʿlā, who related from Saʿīd ibn Jubayr that Ibn ʿAbbās said: The Prophet (ﷺ) said, "*Whoever speaks about the Qur'ān without knowledge then let him take his seat in the Fire.*"[139]

Wakīʿ informed us on the authority of Sufyān from ʿAbdul-Aʿlā al-Thaʿlabī, who related from Saʿīd ibn Jubayr that Ibn ʿAbbās said: The Prophet (ﷺ) said, "*Whoever speaks about the Qur'ān without knowledge then let him take his seat in the Fire.*" Al-Tirmidhī reports from ʿAbd ibn Ḥumayd from Ḥibbān ibn Hilāl, who was informed by Suhayl the brother of Ḥazm al-Qatʿī, who related from Abū ʿImrān al-Jūnī from Jundub that the Prophet (ﷺ) said, "*Whosoever speaks about the Qur'ān using his own intellect and happens to be correct [in his reasoning] is still wrong.*"[140] Al-Tirmidhī declared this *ḥadīth* to be unfamiliar (*gharīb*) and some scholars of *ḥadīth* have spoken concerning Suhayl ibn Abū Ḥazm. These are the reports from the scholars who narrated from the companions of the Prophet (ﷺ) and other than them, all stating the severity of commentating on the Qur'ān without knowledge.

---

[139] *Sunan al-Tirmidhī*, no. 2950.

[140] *Sunan Abu Dawud*, no. 3652 and *Sunan al-Tirmidhī*, no. 2952.

There are some reports that Mujāhid, Qatādah and other than them would commentate on the Qur'ān, however, one does not believe that their commentaries were not based on knowledge or that they spoke of their own desires. There are many narrations from them which support the fact that they did not use their own reasoning in the exegesis of the Qur'ān. Whoever speaks about the Qur'ān using his own reasoning has placed a burden upon himself which he need not bear, and he is treading a path he has not been ordered to tread. Even if he were to stumble upon the correct meaning he would still have erred. The reason for his error is because he did not approach this matter through the correct channel. This is similar to the one who judges between people with ignorance thus ending up in the Fire even if his ruling is correct at times. He is still sinful but his sin is less than the one who is incorrect in his ruling, and Allāh knows best.

The one who strives to reach the truth but then errs still receives a reward; similarly the one who does not strive but then is correct has still erred, especially if what he is discussing contains no room for analogy and reasoning.

When a person commentates on the Qur'ān based on his own reasoning, he may interpret the Qur'ān according to his own views and beliefs, just as the people of desires do. They state that such and such means such and such, referring to what they believe in. Likewise, in later times, those who interpret the Qur'ān with modern and scientific discoveries – even though the Qur'ān does not allude to their interpretations, neither explicitly nor linguistically, have also interpreted the Qur'ān using their own intellect and reasoning; this is impermissible.

Similarly if one does not possess understanding of the linguistic or *sharʿī* meaning of a verse, but still speaks about it, he has also spoken without knowledge, and so is sinful. The example of this is a layman who interprets a verse of the Qur'ān according to his own understanding without any basis, neither linguistic nor *sharʿī*. Such a person has committed an unlawful act. The reason for this is that such a person testifies that this interpretation is what Allāh intended to say, and this is a dangerous matter. Allāh has forbidden that one should speak about Him without knowledge,

قُلْ إِنَّمَا حَرَّمَ رَبِّيَ ٱلْفَوَٰحِشَ مَا ظَهَرَ مِنْهَا وَمَا بَطَنَ وَٱلْإِثْمَ وَٱلْبَغْىَ
بِغَيْرِ ٱلْحَقِّ وَأَن تُشْرِكُوا۟ بِٱللَّهِ مَا لَمْ يُنَزِّلْ بِهِۦ سُلْطَٰنًا وَأَن تَقُولُوا۟
عَلَى ٱللَّهِ مَا لَا تَعْلَمُونَ ﴿٣٣﴾

Say, "My Lord has only forbidden immoralities – what is apparent of them and what is concealed – and sin, and oppression without right, and that you associate with Allāh that for which He has not sent down authority, and that you say about Allāh that which you do not know."

Sūrah al-Aʿrāf, 7:33

Whoever speaks about Allāh without knowledge concerning the meaning of His speech or any of His rulings has committed a grave sin.

Similarly, Allāh refers to the slanderers as liars, as He says,

فَإِذْ لَمْ يَأْتُوا۟ بِٱلشُّهَدَآءِ فَأُو۟لَٰٓئِكَ عِندَ ٱللَّهِ هُمُ ٱلْكَٰذِبُونَ ﴿١٣﴾

And when they do not produce the witnesses, then it is they, in the sight of Allāh, who are the liars.

Sūrah al-Nūr, 24:13

Therefore the slanderer is a liar, even if his slander is relating to an accusation of adultery, for he is spreading what he has no right to spread and speaking about that which he does not possess knowledge of, and Allāh knows best.

It is for this reason that a number of the *salaf* would excuse themselves from interpreting verses they had no knowledge of. This is reported by Shuʿbah from Sulaymān from ʿAbdullāh ibn Murrah, who related from Abū Maʿmar that Abū Bakr al-Ṣiddīq said, 'Which earth will hold me and which sky will shadow me if I speak about the Book of Allāh without knowledge.'[141] It is also reported from Abū ʿUbayd al-Qāsim ibn Salām who narrated from Muḥammad ibn Yazīd from al-ʿAwwām ibn Ḥawshab, who related from Ibrāhīm al-Taymī that Abū Bakr al-Ṣiddīq was asked concerning the verse,

وَفَٰكِهَةً وَأَبًّا ﴿٣١﴾

And fruit and grass

Sūrah ʿAbasa, 80:31

He responded, 'Which sky will shadow me and which earth will hold me if I speak about the Book of Allāh without knowledge.' The chain of narration is disconnected.

If a person was asked concerning the meaning of this previous verse, he may state that the word '*abb*' means father, thus

[141] *Ibn Abī Shaybah*, vol. 6, p. 136.

interpreting the verse according to his own reasoning and ignorance. Since he has heard people saying '*abb*' with an accent (*shaddah*) whereas in reality it is pronounced '*ab*' without an accent, he jumped to the conclusion that this was what the verse was referring to.

Others use the Qur'ānic verses out of context. They use them in places other than where Allāh intended. An example of this is one who is asked about something and responds by quoting the verse,

لَا تَسْـَٔلُوا۟ عَنْ أَشْيَآءَ إِن تُبْدَ لَكُمْ تَسُؤْكُمْ

...do not ask about things which, if they are shown to you, will distress you.

Sūrah al-Mā'idah, 5:101

To use this verse in this context is to use it in a place for which it was not intended.

From here we can also see the error of those who praise the woman who came to be known as, 'the woman who speaks with the Qur'ān'. Her story is mentioned in books of literature. She was a woman who only spoke with the Qur'ān. It is said that for forty years she only spoke with the Qur'ān out of fear of saying something wrong and thus invoking the wrath of Allāh. However, I believe that this act of hers was itself incorrect for by doing this she was using the Qur'ān out of context, and for other than what it was intended.

Abū ʿUbayd narrated that we were informed by Yazīd, who related from Ḥumayd from Anas, that ʿUmar ibn al-Khaṭṭāb recited on the pulpit, ***"And fruit and abbā (grass)."*** 'He asked what is *abb*? As for fruits then we know of them but what is *abb*? He then said to himself, 'Indeed, this is overburdening oneself O ʿUmar."

ʿAbd ibn Ḥumayd reported that Sulaymān ibn Ṣarb narrated from Ibn Zayd, who related from Thābit from Anas who said, 'We were with ʿUmar ibn al-Khaṭṭāb and in his robe were four patches. He recited the verse, *"And fruit and abbā (grass)."* He asked, what is *abb*? He then said, 'Indeed, this is overburdening oneself, what's the harm in not knowing?"

In the portion of the *ḥadīth* in which Anas mentions that ʿUmar had four patches in his robe – is a benefit from the standpoint of the science of *ḥadīth*, as it shows the accuracy of the narrator – the narrator was accurate and aware to the extent that the patches in ʿUmar's clothes did not escape him. In terms of character, it shows the humbleness of the rightly guided caliphs. They considered themselves as one of the people and acted accordingly, to the extent that during the year of the famine ʿUmar forbade himself from eating luxury foods, instead sufficing himself with the least amount of food. All this was to ensure that he did not give preference to himself over others, may Allāh be pleased with him.

That was during a time when the population were upright in their religion and avoided unlawful matters. This is why it is reported that a man said to ʿAlī ibn Abū Ṭālib, 'Why is it that people have revolted against you but they did not revolt against Abū Bakr or ʿUmar?' He replied, "The people in the time of Abū Bakr and ʿUmar were like ʿAlī ibn Abū Ṭālib, and the people in my time are like you."

Likewise, when ʿAbdul-Malik or Hishām ibn ʿAbdul-Malik saw people complaining he gathered their leaders and noblemen and preached to them saying, 'To proceed, if you wish for us to treat you like Abū Bakr or ʿUmar would have, be like the men of the time of Abū Bakr and ʿUmar, and we will treat you like they would have.' It is also often stated, 'As you are, your leaders will be for you.'

All of the above refers to the fact that they (رضي الله عنهما) wanted to discover the reality of the *abb*. Otherwise it is well known to all that it is a type of herbage which grows, as Allāh says,

فَأَنبَتْنَا فِيهَا حَبًّا ﴿٢٧﴾ وَعِنَبًا وَقَضْبًا ﴿٢٨﴾ وَزَيْتُونًا وَنَخْلًا ﴿٢٩﴾ وَحَدَآئِقَ غُلْبًا
﴿٣٠﴾ وَفَٰكِهَةً وَأَبًّا ﴿٣١﴾

And caused to grow within it grain. And grapes and herbage. And olive and palm trees. And gardens of dense shrubbery. And fruit and grass.

Sūrah ʿAbasa, 80:27-31

"And fruits and grass." This is the point of discussion here. Due to the context of the verses, it is obvious that *abb* refers to some form of herbage which grows from the earth. This basic description is not hidden from Abū Bakr and ʿUmar. However, they wished to learn more about it, what it exactly was. What type of herbage is it? This is what confused them. It is said regarding the *abb*, that it is a useful and good form of herbage, possessing much benefit.

Ibn Jarīr narrated from Ya'qūb ibn Ibrāhīm from Ibn 'Ulayyah, who related from Ayyūb from Ibn Abū Mulaykah who stated, 'Ibn 'Abbās was asked concerning some verses – were you to be asked concerning them you would have spoken, but he refused to answer.' Its chain of narration is authentic.

Ibn 'Abbās was the one for whom the Prophet (ﷺ) made *du'ā'* that Allāh should grant him the ability to interpret the Qur'ān. Were this illustrious companion to be asked about a verse he would not reply, unlike many in our times. This illustrates the importance of being cautious when it comes to the exegesis of the Qur'ān.

Abū ʿUbayd narrated from Ismāʿīl ibn Ibrāhīm, who related from Ayyūb from Ibn Abī Mulaykah who said, "A man asked Ibn ʿAbbās about the verse,

يَوْمٍ كَانَ مِقْدَارُهُۥٓ أَلْفَ سَنَةٍ

...a Day, the extent of which is a thousand years.
Sūrah al-Sajdah, 32:5

Ibn ʿAbbās asked him, 'Then what about the verse,

يَوْمٍ كَانَ مِقْدَارُهُۥ خَمْسِينَ أَلْفَ سَنَةٍ ﴿٤﴾

...a Day the extent of which is fifty thousand years."
Sūrah al-Maʿārij, 70:4

The man replied, 'The reason I asked you was so that you would inform me.' Ibn ʿAbbās said, 'They are two days which Allāh has mentioned in His Book, and Allāh knows best what they are [referring to].' He disliked speaking about the Book of Allāh without knowledge."

The duration of the Day of Judgement is fifty thousand years as is in *Sūrah al-Maʿārij*, as Allāh states, ***"...a Day the extent of which is fifty thousand years. So be patient with gracious patience."*** This is also confirmed by the Prophet (ﷺ) in the *ḥadīth* of Abū Hurayrah collected by Muslim,[142] in which it is mentioned that the one who refused to pay the *zakāh* will be punished on a Day, the length of which is fifty thousand years.

As for the verse in *Sūrah al-Sajdah*, ***"...a Day, the extent of which is a thousand years"*** then this – and Allāh knows best – refers to this world. The context of the verse states, ***"He arranges [each] matter from the heaven to the earth; then it will ascend to Him in a Day, the extent of which is a thousand years of***

[142] *Sahih Muslim*, no. 987.

those which you count." The 'day' in the verse, ***"And indeed, a day with your Lord is like a thousand years of those which you count"***[143] is described as being with Allāh, hence we cannot speculate concerning its reality, Allāh knows best concerning it.

---

[143] Sūrah Ḥajj, 22:47.

Ibn Jarīr narrated from Ya'qūb ibn Ibrāhīm from Ibn 'Ulayyah, who related from Mahdī ibn Maymūn from al-Walīd ibn Muslim who said, 'Ṭalaq ibn Ḥabīb came to Jundub ibn Abdullāh[144] and asked him concerning a verse of the Qur'ān. He replied, "I implore you never to come to me if you are a Muslim." And in a narration he said, "...never to sit with me."'

This is from piety and refraining from speaking about the meanings of the Qur'ān. The point isn't to say to everyone who asks you concerning a verse 'don't sit with me.' Rather, this was to stress how careful one should be in these matters.

[144] Jundub ibn 'Abdullāh al-Bajalī was one of the companions of the Prophet (ﷺ). He died between 60 and 70 AH.

Mālik narrated from Yaḥyā ibn Sa'īd that if Sa'īd ibn al-Musayyib was ever asked concerning a verse of the Qur'ān he would say, 'We do not say anything concerning the [*tafsīr* of the] Qur'ān.'

Al-Layth reported from Yaḥyā ibn Sa'īd that Sa'īd ibn al-Musayyib would not speak except about that which he knew when it came to the Qur'ān.

Shu'bah related from 'Amr ibn Murrah who said, "A man asked Sa'īd ibn al-Musayyib about a verse of the Qur'ān and he replied, 'Do not ask me concerning the Qur'ān. Rather ask the one who claims that none of it is hidden from him.' He was referring to 'Ikrimah."

Ibn Shawdhab reports from Yazīd ibn Abū Yazīd who said, 'We would ask Sa'īd ibn al-Musayyib about the lawful (*ḥalāl*) and unlawful (*ḥarām*) and he was the most knowledgeable concerning these matters. Then when we would ask him about the *tafsīr* of a verse, and he would remain silent as if he had not heard us.'

Ibn Jarīr narrated from Aḥmad ibn 'Abdah al-Ḍabbī, who related from Ḥammād ibn Zayd from 'Ubaydullāh ibn 'Umar who said, 'I have met the jurists of Madīnah and they considered it a grave matter to speak about *tafsīr*. From them was Sālim ibn 'Abdullāh,[145] al-Qāsim ibn Muḥammad,[146] Sa'īd ibn al-Musayyib and Nāfi'.[147]'

Abū 'Ubayd reported from 'Abdullāh ibn Ṣāliḥ, who related from al-Layth from Hishām ibn 'Urwah who said, 'I never heard my father interpret a verse from the Qur'ān.'

---

[145] Sālim ibn 'Abdullāh ibn 'Umar, died 106 AH. He was one of the distinguished jurists of Madīnah.

[146] Al-Qāsim ibn Muḥammad, the grandson of Abū Bakr. He was a great scholar of *ḥadīth* and *fiqh* who died in 106 AH.

[147] Abū 'Abdullāh Nāfi', died 117 AH. He was the free slave of Ibn 'Umar, a renowned scholar of *ḥadīth* and *fiqh*. He was sent to Egypt as a teacher by 'Umar ibn 'Abdul-'Azīz.

Ayyūb, Ibn ʿAwn and Hishām al-Dastawā'ī all reported from Muḥammad ibn Sīrīn that he said, 'I asked ʿUbaydah al-Salmānī concerning a verse of the Qur'ān. He replied, "Those who knew in which circumstances the verses were revealed have passed away. Rather fear Allāh and remain firm and upright."'

Abū ʿUbayd reported from Muʿādh from Ibn ʿAwn, who related from ʿUbaydullāh ibn Muslim ibn Yasār[148] from his father who said, 'Before you speak about Allāh, pause and look at what precedes and follows it [i.e. look at the context].'

Hushaym narrated from Mughīrah from Ibrāhīm[149] who said, 'Our peers used to try to avoid [having to] explain verses and would give [this science] much respect.'

Shuʿbah narrated from ʿAbdullāh ibn Abū al-Safar, that al-Shaʿbī said, 'I swear by Allāh, there is not a single verse except that I have asked concerning it, but it [*tafsīr*] is to narrate from Allāh.'

Abū ʿUbayd narrated from Hushaym who narrated from ʿUmar ibn Abū Zā'idah, who related from al-Shaʿbī from Masrūq who said, 'Beware of *tafsīr*, for indeed it is reporting from Allāh.'

These and other authentic narrations from the pious predecessors all state the impermissibility of speaking about *tafsīr* without knowledge. However, there is no harm in speaking [about *tafsīr*] if one possesses the relevant linguistic and religious knowledge.

It is for this reason that there are a number of varying statements reported from these scholars. This does not imply contradiction, for they spoke about matters they had knowledge of, and remained silent on that which they had no knowledge of. This is what is obligatory upon everyone. Just as one should remain

[148] Muslim ibn Yāsir al-Baṣrī, died 100 AH. He was originally from Makkah but later settled in Basrah, and distinguished himself as a scholar of *ḥadīth* and *fiqh*.

[149] Ibrāhīm ibn Yazīd ibn Qays al-Nakhaʿī, died 96 AH. He was one of the most eminent *tābiʿīn*. He became a distinguished scholar of *fiqh* and was known as the jurist of Iraq.

quiet about that which he is ignorant of, likewise he should speak about that which he possesses knowledge of when he is asked concerning it, as Allāh says:

لَتُبَيِّنُنَّهُۥ لِلنَّاسِ وَلَا تَكْتُمُونَهُۥ

...You must make it clear [i.e. explain it] to the people and not conceal it.

Sūrah Āl-ʿImrān, 3:187

This is also due to what is reported in the *ḥadīth*, ***"Whosoever is asked about a matter but conceals it, will be given a bridle of fire on the Day of Judgement."***

Ibn Jarīr reported from Muḥammad ibn Bashār from Mu'ammal, who related from Sufyān from Abū al-Zinād that Ibn ʿAbbās said, '*Tafsīr* is of four types; a type which the Arabs know from their language, a type which no-one is allowed to be ignorant of, a type which is known to the scholars and a type which is not known except to Allāh.' And Allāh knows best.

These are the four types: a type of *tafsīr* known to the Arabs from their language. This includes words such as cave, (*al-kahf*), throne (*ʿarsh*), layered with fruit (*mandūd*), banana tree (*talḥ*) and so on. A type of *tafsīr* which everyone must know and no-one is excused from such as what one must know regarding matters of belief and action. An example is the verse, ***"...establish the prayer"***. Each person must know what this establishment of prayer consists of. Likewise, each person must be aware of the fundamental parts of belief such as faith in the Messengers. The third type of *tafsīr* is that which the scholars are aware of, the general, specific, restricted and unrestricted, as well as the abrogated and the rulings related to all this. Not everyone possesses knowledge of this third type nor is it obligatory upon everyone to do so, rather it is a collective obligation. The last type of *tafsīr* is a type known only to Allāh. Whoever claims knowledge of this type is a liar as is mentioned in some narrations. Examples include knowledge of the reality of the attributes of Allāh, the affairs of the Day of Judgement, Paradise, the Fire, and such affairs of the unseen. Whosoever claims knowledge of these affairs is a liar. Such knowledge is only with Allāh.

Summary

A Summary of '*An Introduction to the Principles of Tafsīr*'

1. Knowledge is either a narration from an infallible source, or a statement supported by clear proof. All else is either fabricated and thus rejected, or its status as acceptable or unacceptable is unknown.

2. It is obligatory to know that the Prophet (ﷺ) explained the meanings of the Qur'ān to his companions just as he taught them its words. The statement of Allāh, ***"...that you may make clear to the people what was sent down to them..."***[150] includes both these aspects.

3. The nobler the generation, the greater the knowledge, understanding, unity and co-operation present amongst its people.

4. The pious predecessors (*salaf*) rarely differed in *tafsīr*. Their differences of opinion in practical rulings are much greater than their differences in *tafsīr*. That which is classed as differences of opinion are more variations in wording than they are contradictions. These are of two categories:

[150] Sūrah al-Naḥl, 16:44.

The first category is the expression of one and the same idea by using different words. An example of this is referring to the same concept by one person mentioning a particular aspect concerning it and another mentioning another aspect. These explanations are like using equivalent names which lie between synonyms and antonyms.

5. Every single name of Allāh refers to Him and the attributes that name possesses. By necessity, it also refers to the attributes which other names may possess. This is a principle when discussing the names and attributes of Allāh.

6. If the intention of the questioner is to pinpoint an object, it can be described using any name so long as it is understood to refer to that particular object.

7. If the intention of the questioner is to learn about the attribute which that name connotes, an added explanation must also be given. For example, a person may ask concerning the names of Allāh: *al-Quddūs* (the Pure), *al-Salām* (the Perfect), *al-Mu'min* (the Bestower of faith) whilst knowing that these names refer to Allāh, however, the questioner wishes to inquire about these specific attributes.

8. If that which has proceeded is clear, one realises that it is often the case that the predecessors (*salaf*) would describe something using a name which points to the object being referred to; at the same time this name may also contain an attribute not present in its other names. It is well-known that this is not a contradictory difference as some people mistakenly think.

The only point of difference is concerning a general term which is used in a particular case; is it limited to that case or not? None of the Muslim scholars infer that the general terms present in the Qur'ān and *Sunnah* only pertain to those specific people about whom those verses were revealed. Rather, the most that can be said is that such said verses apply to all those who are similar to that person for which the verse was revealed, and the wording is not generalised to the limits to which the language allows. Any verse which was revealed for a particular reason, especially if the verse is an order or a prohibition, not only includes that particular person for whom it was revealed but all those similar to him. This is also the case if the verse is praising or censuring someone.

9. Their statement: 'This verse was revealed due to such and such' can sometimes mean that this was the reason the verse was revealed. It can also imply that this meaning is also present in the verse even if it is not the reason for its revelation, i.e. the meaning of this verse is such and such.

10. If one mentions a reason for which the verse was revealed and then another mentions a different reason, it is possible that both are speaking the truth and that the verse was revealed after a number of incidents took place, or the verse was revealed twice; on each occasion for a different reason. Another type of difference which can be found is where we have equivocal words. This is because it has a number of meanings in the language such as the word '*qaswarah*' which can refer to a shooter or a lion, and the word "*as'asa*' which can refer to both the advent and departure of the night. Or it may be because even though the word originally only has one meaning, it denotes one of two different types or one of two things such as a pronominal subject, like in the verse: ***"Then he approached and descended. And was at a distance of two bow lengths or nearer."***[151] There are very few words in the Arabic language which are synonymous; this is even rarer in the Qur'ān if not non-existent.

11. It is common for the Arabs to attach a verb to another verb by using the preposition of the latter. As such, we can see the mistake made by those who substitute certain words with others.

[151] Sūrah al-Najm, 53:8-9.

12. Differences of opinion may occur due to relevant evidences being hidden, overlooked, not being known or being misunderstood, or due to one favouring an opposing opinion.

13. Differences in the exegesis of the Qur'ān can be of two types: The source of the first is narrations and the other type is derived from different means, for knowledge is either a truthful narration, or a correct deduction, and the narrations either originate from one who is infallible or one who is not.

The purpose is to discuss these narrations irrespective of whether they stem from an infallible authority or not; this is the first category. At times, we are able to distinguish between authentic and weak narrations and at times we are unable to do so. The second category whose authenticity we cannot ascertain, for the most part is unbeneficial and to delve into it is unnecessary. As for that knowledge which is essential to the Muslims, Allāh has placed for them sufficient signs showing them the truth.

14. When the narrations of the *tābiʿūn* differ, some of their sayings do not possess greater authority than others. Rather, authentic narrations from the companions in this regard are more reliable than narrations from their students.

15. The first category in which one is able to establish the authenticity of a narration is possible – and all praise is for Allāh – in those matters which are essential.

16. The point here is that there are clear signs showing the authenticity or weakness of those narrations which are essential and required by the Muslims.

17. *Mursal ḥadīths* which are reported by many narrators to the extent that there can be no chance of intentional or incidental collusion between the narrators are without doubt authentic.

18. Using this method, it is possible to determine the authenticity of narrations which are reported through different transmissions,

even though each individual narration is not sufficient on its own due to a missing link present or the weakness of a narrator.

19. This is an essential principal to remember, and is very beneficial in determining the truthfulness of narrations in *ḥadīth*, *tafsīr* and military expeditions, and what people said or did.

20. The point is that if a *ḥadīth* has been narrated from two different chains without collaboration, it cannot be a mistake or a lie.

21. The majority of what is in *Bukhārī* and *Muslim* can be ascribed to the Prophet (ﷺ) with certainty, as it is of a high calibre.

22. The majority of scholars from all of the different schools of thought agree that if a *ḥadīth* reported with a single narrator in its chain of narration is accepted or approved by action, then it is sufficient as evidence.

23. Just as they use the *ḥadīths* of the one with bad memory as supporting evidence, they [scholars of *ḥadīth*] may also classify the *ḥadīth* of a trustworthy and reliable narrator as weak due to apparent and clear errors found in certain narrations. This is known as the science of *ʿilal al-ḥadīth* (the hidden defects in *ḥadīth*), and it is one of the most noble and advanced sciences in this field.

24. People are of two extremes in this issue. A group of scholastic theologians and their likes who are unfamiliar with the science of *ḥadīth* and its scholars do not differentiate between authentic and weak narrations. This causes them to doubt the authenticity of *ḥadīths* even though they are classified as authentic by the scholars of this science. The other group claims to follow *ḥadīths* wherever they find a wording narrated by a trustworthy person, or a *ḥadīth* which appears to be authentic, considering it to be from among those *ḥadīths* whose authenticity has been established by the scholars. Even if they contradict a well known and authentic *ḥadīth*, they will revert to facile interpretations or insist it is an

evidence for a certain issue even though the scholars of *ḥadīth* consider it to be incorrect. Just as there are signs by which one can come to know and establish that a ḥadīth is truthful, likewise there are signs which also point to a *ḥadīth* being a fabrication.

25. In the books of *tafsīr*, many such fabrications exist, such as the *ḥadīth* narrated by al-Thaʿabī, al-Wāḥidī and al-Zamakhsharī regarding the superiority of the chapters of the Qur'ān. These are fabricated by the agreement of the scholars.

26. The second of the two categories in which differences occur relates to reasoning and deduction as opposed to narrations. Most mistakes which occur in *tafsīr* are as a result of two things which appeared after the generation of the companions, their students (*tābiʿūn*) and those who followed them in righteousness.

27. The first problem which arose was people believing in certain ideologies and then interpreting the Qur'ān to fit those ideologies. The second problem was a group of people who interpreted the Qur'ān just as an average Arabic speaker would, without considering from whom these words came, to whom it was revealed and who they were addressing.

28. The first group [achieves its objective] by employing two methods; either by stripping the words of the Qur'ān of their real and intended meanings, or by giving the words meanings which they do not convey. In both methods, that which they wish to affirm or negate can be incorrect and thus they are mistaken in the evidence used and that which they want to support.

29. The point being made here is that this group of people held certain beliefs and then interpreted the words of the Qur'ān in support of those beliefs. In this regard, they have no predecessors from the companions, their students (*tābiʿūn*) or those who followed them from the great scholars of the Muslims, neither in their beliefs nor in their commentaries of the Qur'ān.

30. From amongst them are individuals who are eloquent and charming, and are able to conceal their innovations so that most people will not realise, such as the author of *Kashāf* and others. This particular author manages to confuse many who would not expect him to possess erroneous views.

31. In short, whoever diverts away from the methodology of the companions, their students and their commentaries to what opposes them is wrong in this. Rather he is an innovator in this respect, even though he may be striving to attain the truth and so be forgiven for his errors.

32. Thus, whosoever opposes their statements possesses certain doubts, either intellectual or textual, as has been expounded upon elsewhere.

33. Here, we wish to highlight the causes of difference in *tafsīr*. One of the greatest causes is innovation and falsehood whose proponents go to the extent of distorting the words of Allāh, and interpreting the statements of Allāh and His Messenger (ﷺ) incorrectly and twisting their meanings.

34. Those who err in their deductions and not their methods are like the *Ṣūfīs*, preachers, jurists and others who interpret the Qur'ān with correct ideas but the words of the Qur'ān do not imply such meanings.

35. The most authentic method with which to explain the Qur'ān is with the Qur'ān. If you are unable to do this, then use the *Sunnah*.

36. If you do not find the *tafsīr* in the Qur'ān or *Sunnah* you return to the statements of the companions.

37. Israelite traditions are of three types: a type which is authentic as its truthfulness is attested to by our own sources, a type which is false as our own sources reject it, and a third type which does not fall into the previous two categories. We can neither judge

it to be authentic or inauthentic; as such we neither believe in it nor reject it. One is allowed to quote from this third type, even though most of what is contained in it is of no immediate religious benefit.

38. The best way of mentioning differences of opinion is to gather all of the relevant opinions, mention the correct opinion while refuting the incorrect and then stating the fruit and benefit derived from the discussion. This is to ensure that one does not prolong discussion over insignificant matters which possess no benefit and one does not divert from what is more crucial and important.

One who does not gather all the different opinions on a particular issue has presented an incomplete argument, as the truth may lie in what he has neglected. Similarly, the one who does not point out the correct opinion has also performed an incomplete task. If one intentionally authenticates something incorrect, he has ascribed lies and falsehood, and if one does this out of ignorance then he has erred.

Similarly, whoever discusses differences in issues which hold little or no benefit, or mentions varying opinions which even though they possess different wordings all dissolve into just one or two opinions has wasted time and has incorrectly exaggerated the matter. Such a person is like one who wears two robes, both of which are stolen.

39. If scholars are unable to find the explanation of a verse in the Qur'ān or *Sunnah*, and do not find any relevant commentaries from the companions, then many of the scholars use the statements of the successors (*tābiʿūn*).

40. Shuʿbah ibn Ḥajjāj and others have said that the statements of the successors in matters such as practical rulings are not authoritative, so how can they be so in issues of *tafsīr*? This means that their opinions are not authoritative over other [successors] who hold contrary views; this is true. However, if they all agree on a single issue then without doubt it is sufficient as evidence.

41. Exegesis of the Qur'ān based only on one's reasoning is *ḥarām*.

42. Whoever speaks about the Qur'ān using his own reasoning has placed a burden upon himself which he need not bear. He is also treading a path he has not been ordered to tread. Even if he were to stumble upon the correct meaning, he would still have erred. The reason for his error is because he did not approach this matter through its proper avenue. This is similar to the one who judges between people with ignorance. His end is in the Fire even if at times his ruling is correct, thus he is still sinful but his sin is less than the one who is incorrect in his ruling, and Allāh knows best.

43. These and other authentic narrations from the pious predecessors all state the impermissibility of speaking about *tafsīr* without knowledge. However, there is no harm in speaking [about *tafsīr*] if one possesses the required linguistic and religious knowledge. It is for this reason that there are a number of varying statements reported from these scholars. This does not imply contradiction, for they spoke about matters they had knowledge of, and remained silent on that which they had no knowledge of.

Glossary

Aḥkām: Sing: *ḥukm*. A law or judgement. In the *sharīʿah*, the most important kind is the assignment of a value to human actions: obligatory, prohibited, praiseworthy, disliked or neutral.

Asbāb al-nuzūl: The circumstances which led to the revelation of a particular verse or passage of the Qur'ān.

Ashʿarī: An Islamic sect founded in the third century of *Hijrah*. From their beliefs is that *īmān* is only belief (i.e., actions are not part of *īmān*); that *īmān* does not increase or decrease; that *tawḥīd* is restricted to affirming the perfect nature of Allāh (i.e., *Rubūbiyyah*); and that most of the attributes of Allāh are metaphorical.

ʿĀshūrā: The tenth day of the Islamic month of *Muḥarram*. It is recommended to fast on that day, along with the day before or the day after.

Daʿwah: Lit: 'an invitation'; Islamically, it refers to the invitation to Islam, or more generally, the propogation of any religion or belief system.

Fatwā: A religious edict or verdict.

Fiqh: Lit: 'understanding'; Islamically, it refers to knowledge of the detailed laws of the *Sharīʿah* related to people's actions, along with the detailed evidence for those laws.

Gharīb: Lit: strange/unfamiliar. This is when there is a single narrator in one of the stages of transmission.

Ḥadīth: A report about the Prophet; his statement, action or tacit approval of actions of his Companions, or description of his physical appearance or character.

Ḥalāl: Permissible; one of the five classifications of human actions, according to the *sharīʿah*.

Ḥarām: Prohibited; one of the five classifications of human actions, according to the *sharīʿah*.

Iḥrām: A state of consecration entered into when one intends to perform *Ḥajj* or *ʿUmrah*. Certain normally lawful acts become prohibited.

Isnād: The chain of narrators for a *ḥadīth*, by which the reliability of a text may be judged.

Isrā'īliyāt: Reports of the Jews and Christians about religious issues and events. The Prophet permitted Muslims to transmit these reports, which fall into three categories: reports confirmed by the Qur'ān and *Sunnah*, which we thus know to be true; reports contradicted by the Qur'ān and *Sunnah*, which we know to be false; reports containing information about which the Qur'ān and *Sunnah* are silent. We can neither confirm nor deny this last category.

Jaḥmiyyah: The first markedly philosophical heretical sect in Islam; followers of Jaḥm ibn Ṣafwān. They denied all of Allāh's attributes.

Kalālah: A case related to the rulings of inheritance; in this case the deceased leaves neither descendants nor ascendants as heirs.

Khawārij: The first sect to split ranks with the Muslims. They believed that any person who committed a major sin, such as stealing, lying, or fornicating, became a disbeliever due to that sin. They considered most of the companions to be disbelievers, and as such fought them.

Khuṭbah al-Ḥājjah: Lit: sermon of need. This was the sermon with which the Prophet would begin all of his sermons.

Liʿān: Lit: curse. These are the four sworn testimonies taken by a man who accuses his wife of adultery. This is accompanied by a fifth testimony in which the wrath and curse of Allāh is invoked upon the liar. The wife can counteract these testimonies by making five similar testimonies of her own after which the husband and wife are separated and can never remarry.

Muʿaṭṭilah: Those who fall into *taʿṭīl*; to deny all or some of the attributes of Allāh.

Madhab: It is most frequently used for the schools of thought in Islamic law; the four major ones being the Ḥanafī, Mālikī, Shāfiʿī and Ḥanbalī schools.

Muḍtarib: A disordered *ḥadīth* in which a number of reports with the same strength differ; thus, neither compromise nor abrogation nor preponderance can be applied.

Murji'ah: An Islamic deviant sect which holds the belief that sins do not harm believers just as good deeds do not benefit disbelievers. They also leave the position of those who commit major sins to Allāh in the Hereafter.

Mursal: An incomplete transmission. A *ḥadīth* whose chain of transmission lacks a Companion transmitter. In other words it refers to a *ḥadīth* in which a *tābiʿī* has directly narrated from the Prophet without the mention of a Companion as a link between him and the Prophet.

Musharrakah: A case related to the rulings of inheritance; this is when the deceased is survived by a husband, mother, two or more maternal brothers and any number of full brothers.

Mutābiʿ: A *ḥadīth* whose wording or meaning is identical to another *hadīth* which is also reported by the same Companion.

Muʿtazillah: A rationalist Islamic sect. They figuratively interpreted texts about Allāh's attributes or denied them outright. They also denied large portions of the *Sunnah*, affirmed absolute human free will, and considered sinful Muslims to be eternally doomed to Hell. This was all as a result of their giving precedence to their deductions over the texts of the Qur'ān and *Sunnah*.

Qadr: The pre-decree of Allāh.

Qiyās: A legal analogy by which a law is extended from a case mentioned in a text of the Qur'ān or *Sunnah* to a case for which there is no specific text on the basis of the same effective cause for the law in both cases.

Rāfiḍah: The name applied to the Twelver *Shī'ite* sect, so called since they believe in twelve *Imāms*. They ascribe powers of lordship to these *Imāms*, perform *ṭawāf* around their graves and direct their *duʿās* to them.

Ṣaḥīḥ: Lit: authentic; in *ḥadīth* terminology, it means a rigorously authenticated report, whose *isnād* is connected, whose narrators are of good charater and accurate memory, and which is free from hidden defects or contradiction with more authentic texts.

Salaf: The pious predecessors; normally referring to the first three generations of Muslims.

Shaddah: The doubling of consonants.

Shāhid: A *ḥadīth* whose wording or meaning is identical to another *ḥadīth*, but the narrating Companion is different in both.

Sharīʿah: The divinely revealed law contained in the Qur'ān and the *Sunnah*. It is comprehensive in its scope, covering issues of belief, devotional worship, and personal interactions as well as commercial, criminal, constitutional and international law.

Shīʿah: The term applied to a variety of dissident groups united in their belief that the Prophet's cousin ʿAlī ibn Abū Ṭālib and his descendants were divinely appointed to lead the Muslims spiritually and politically.

Ṣūfī: An adherent of *Ṣūfism*, a mystical interpretation of Islām that stresses the primary importance of rememberance of Allāh as well as the necessity of submitting one's will to a spiritual guide in order to progress spiritually. Latter-day *Ṣūfī* doctrines such as *waḥdat al-wujūd* (the unity of being) and *fanā'* (nirvana) owe more to Buddhism and Hinduism than they do to Islām.

Sūrah: Plural: *suwar*; A chapter of the Qur'ān.

Tābiʿūn: The second generation of Muslims. They are those who met the Companions of the Prophet.

Tafsīr: Lit: interpretation, Islamically, it is the science of explaining the meanings of the Qur'ān.

Ṭawāf: An act of worship which consists of circumumbulating the *Kaʿbah* seven times.

Tawḥīd: The Islamic concept of monotheism. It consists of unifying Allāh in His Lordship, His right of worship and His Names and Attributes.

Ummah: The group of people to whom a prophet is sent. The more common meaning of the Muslim *Ummah* is those people who have believed in the Prophet Muḥammad.

Uṣūl ul-Fiqh: The principles of Islamic jurisprudence; a system of rules developed by generations of Islamic scholars for the correct deduction of laws from the texts of the Qur'ān and *Sunnah*.

Zakāh: An annual obligatory charity taken from Muslims possessing a fixed amount of wealth and distributed among the poor and several other categories of recipients.

Ẓihār: The statement of a husband to his wife "You are to me like the back of my mother" or such similar statements, i.e. unlawful for me to approach sexually. This was a type of separation practiced by the Arabs in pre-Islām in which the wife was neither explicitly divorced nor married. As such Islām abolished it.